WESTERN HEMISPHERE.

WHAT DARWIN SAW

CHARLES DARWIN.

WHAT DARWIN SAW

IN HIS VOYAGE ROUND THE WORLD
IN THE SHIP *BEAGLE*

THE *BEAGLE* LAID ASHORE AT THE MOUTH OF THE SANTA CRUZ

WEATHERVANE BOOKS
NEW YORK

To

The Great Name of

Charles Darwin

Originally published, in 1879, as *What Mr. Darwin Saw in His Voyage Round the World in the ship* Beagle.

This edition is published by Weathervane Books, distributed by Crown Publishers, Inc.

b c d e f g h

Library of Congress Cataloging in Publication Data
Darwin, Charles Robert, 1809-1882.
What Mr. Darwin saw in his voyage round the world in the ship Beagle.
Compiled from the author's Journal of researches into the geology and natural history of the various countries visited by the H.M.S. Beagle.
Reprint of the 1879 ed. published by Harper, New York.
Includes indexes.
1. Natural history. 2. South America—Description and travel. 3. Beagle expedition, 1831-1836. I. Title.
QH11.D236 1978 500.9′8 78-12018
ISBN 0-517-26310-6

FOR PARENTS.

THE design of this book can be stated in a few words, namely, to interest children in the study of natural history, and of physical and political geography.

I. It would be hard to find a child indifferent to stories about animals. The number of books, both systematic and unsystematic, to which this fact has given rise is very large; but the enormous progress in zoological science has been fatal to the survival of most of them. Children of a prior generation had their curiosity about the brute creation satisfied by White's *Selborne* and Bewick's *Quadrupeds;* and the former classic is even now reprinted in popular editions, with illustrations which may and do attract the young. But adults, and even scholars, alone can enjoy *Selborne* to the full; while not merely is the *Quadrupeds* out of print and difficult to procure, but its text is too antiquated to be usefully put before a child. Its incomparable illustrations deserve a perpetual lease of life. The first section of the present compilation, entitled "Animals," though written more than forty years ago, will, it is confidently believed, be as fresh and trustworthy forty years hence as it is now.

The compiler has thought it an advantage to connect stories about a great variety of animals with one person, and he an observer of such credibility and authority that little if anything that was learned of him would have to be unlearned. Mr. Darwin was, of course, pre-eminently such an observer. On the other hand, by carefully connecting these stories also with the places on the earth's surface where the animals were studied, a correct notion will be had of the distribution of the animal kingdom, with a corresponding insight into the geography of the globe in its broadest sense. Finally, by placing these stories first in order, the attention of the youngest readers is assured. No artificial grouping has been attempted.

II. Scarcely inferior in interest to tales of animals are accounts of strange peoples and customs, particularly of savage and barbarous life. The section entitled "Man," therefore, should not disappoint the youthful reader.

III. Closely allied with the foregoing are the contents of the section entitled (for want of a better designation) "Geography," which consists partly of descriptions of cities, the habitations of man, partly of descriptions of rivers, mountains, valleys, plains, and other physical features of the countries visited by Mr. Darwin.

IV. Finally, in the section styled "Nature" will be found some account of the grander terrestrial processes and phenomena, with other matters which a strict classification might have placed in the preceding section, but which were intentionally reserved till the last, as being least easy to comprehend. But experience may show that, on the whole, this is far from being the least interesting of the four.

From what has been said, it will be perceived that, if the attempted gradation has been successful, this book recommends itself to every member of a household, from the youngest to the oldest. A child may safely be left to read as far as he is interested, or as far as he can understand with facility, in the certainty that each year afterward he will push his explorations a little further, till the end has been reached and the whole is within his grasp. Meantime, parents can read aloud selected passages even in advance of the child's progress. Nor does the compiler seem to himself to overrate his collection of excerpts when he suggests its use as a graded reader in schools. Its capacity for rhetorical exercise will be found greater than might have been expected, and those who have been led to believe Mr. Darwin a materialist will discover here eloquent expression of human sympathies as broad as those immortalized by the old Roman comedian—"Homo sum, humani nil a me alienum puto."

Some liberties have been taken with the original text. Notices of the same animal, or place, or nationality, or phenomenon, in different parts of the narrative, have been gathered together and pieced where necessary; and (always after much hesitation) a more simple word or phrase has occasionally been substituted for a less simple. But the amount of these additions and alterations is relatively so slight that it is true to say that Mr. Darwin speaks throughout. A few of the illustrations are borrowed from the original narrative and from its sister reports; but by far the greater number have been derived from other sources, and all with a view to conveying correct information. The maps interspersed with the text or placed at the end of the volume contain every significant geographical name mentioned in the text.

After all, it is hoped that every one who here learns for the first time a small portion of "what Mr. Darwin saw," on his memorable first journey abroad, will sooner or later betake himself to the delightful and ever wonderful unabridged report of the most momentous voyage round the world since Columbus.

New York, *October* 1, 1879.

FOR CHILDREN.

EVERYBODY has eyes, but, as you know, some people are blind; and many of those who are not blind wear glasses, and cannot see without them. But even those whose eyes are good and strong do not all see alike. In a roomful of people, you would be sure to see your father and mother; and if all the rest were strangers to you, you would probably not notice a good many of them. Or if you were just learning to read, and were shown a printed page, you would see the words you know how to spell, and would pay very little attention to most of the others. If we should go searching for spring flowers, I, who know what anemones and hepaticas are like, should find more than you who had never seen them before. And if our walk was among woods, some would come home remembering only that they had seen trees; others, that they had seen pines and oaks; and I alone, perhaps, that I had seen birches and ash trees too. And again, if our excursion was by roads you had never travelled before, some of you could next time go the same way without my showing you, while others would feel lost at the first turn.

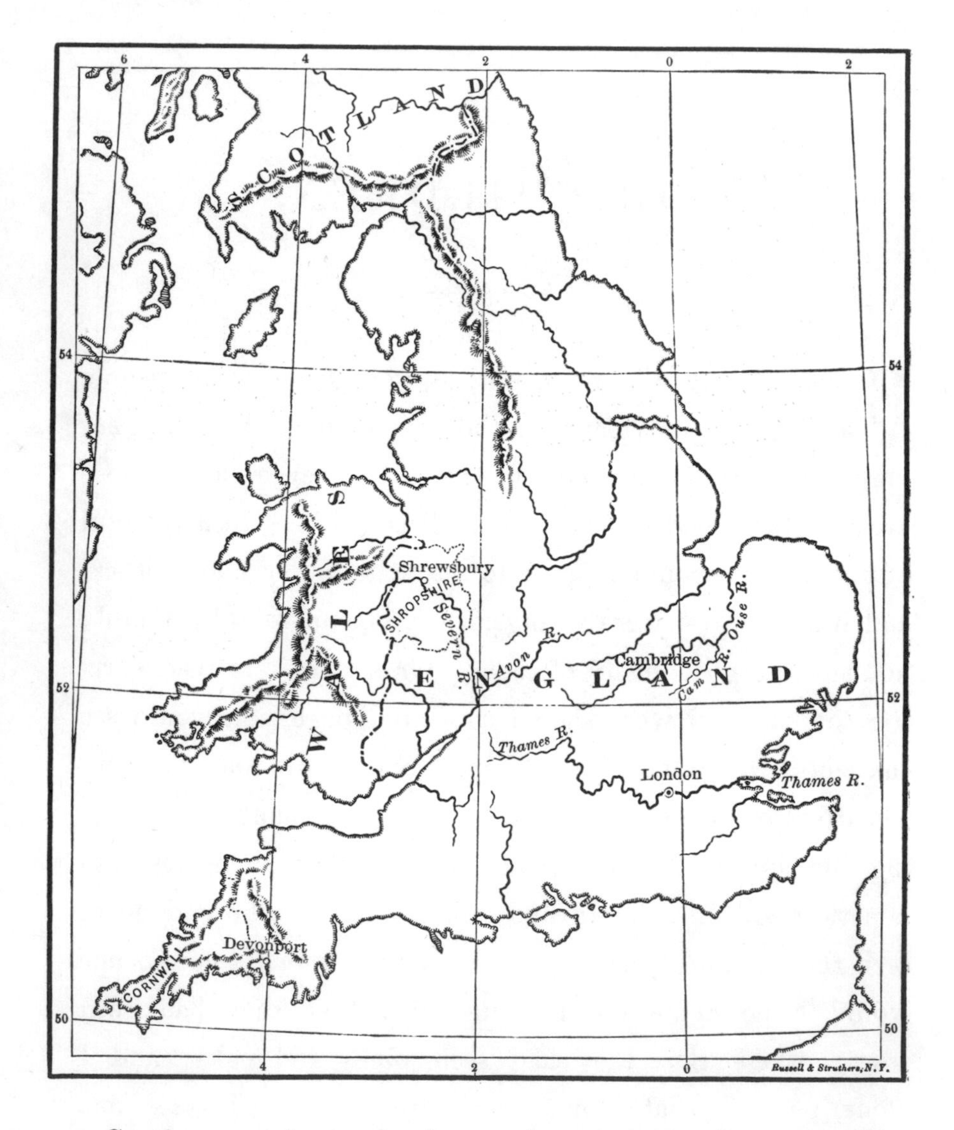

So those see best who know the most, or who naturally take notice of new things. Now Charles Darwin, about

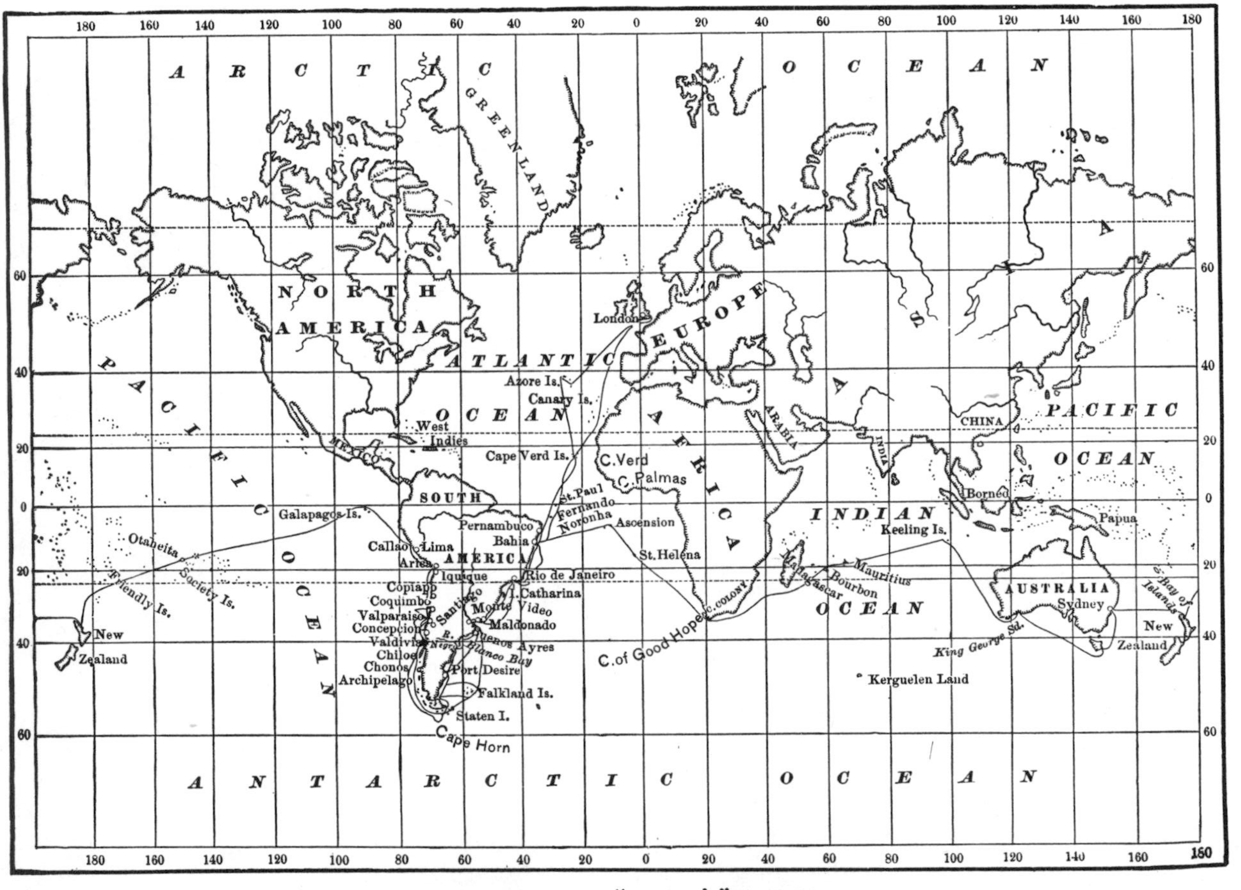

CHART OF THE "BEAGLE'S" VOYAGE.

whom I am going to tell you presently, was one of the best seers that ever lived, partly because he had learned so well what to look for, and partly because nothing escaped his eyes. Before he himself travelled, he read a great many books of travel, and he seemed to remember at the right time just what it was useful for him to remember. But before that, he had trained himself, with the aid of the microscope, to observe little things; and people have not yet got over their astonishment at learning how many important things he thus saw which they had never seen, or had seen without thinking them of any consequence. And now all the world looks at things differently from what it used to before he showed it how. *How* he saw things you will partly see by reading the following pages, taken from his account of the voyage of the *Beagle*.

Charles Darwin (whose full name was Charles Robert Darwin) was born at Shrewsbury, a famous town in Shrop shire, England, February 12, 1809. His father was Dr. Robert Waring Darwin; his grandfather Dr. Erasmus Darwin, also a distinguished naturalist. His mother's father was Josiah Wedgwood, the celebrated manufacturer of pottery, some of which goes by his name. Mr. Darwin was educated, first at Shrewsbury, then at the University of Edinburgh, and finally at Christ's College, Cambridge. The end of his schooling was in 1831. Then Captain Fitzroy invited him to join the *Beagle* as naturalist, and he sailed from Devonport, England, December 27, 1831, not to return till October

22, 1836. The object of the expedition was principally "to complete the survey of Patagonia and Tierra del Fuego, commenced under Captain King in 1826 to 1830, and to survey

THE KINGDOM OF ÆSOP.

the shores of Chili, Peru, and of some islands in the Pacific," besides sailing round the world. The first Christmas-day spent away from England (1832) was at St. Martin's Cove, near Cape Horn; the second (1833), at Port Desire, in Patagonia; the third (1834), in a wild harbor in the peninsula of Tres Montes, also in Patagonia; the fourth and last (1835), at the Bay of Islands, New Zealand. The map facing page 17 will show you the course of the expedition. Mr. Darwin died April 19, 1882.

Before beginning to read "What Mr. Darwin Saw," try how good a seer you are by counting the various animals shown in the wood-engraving on the opposite page, by the great Thomas Bewick.

CONTENTS.

ANIMALS.

MAN.

GEOGRAPHY.

NATURE.

ILLUSTRATIONS.

MAPS AND CHARTS.

I.

ANIMALS.

WHAT DARWIN SAW

THE HORSE.

URUGUAY.

I ONCE crossed the River Santa Lucia near its mouth, and was surprised to observe how easily our horses, although not used to swim, passed over a width of at least six hundred yards. On mentioning this at Montevideo, I was told that a vessel containing some mountebanks and their horses being wrecked in the Plata, one horse swam seven miles to the shore. In the course of the day I was amused by the skill with which a Gaucho forced a restive horse to swim a river. He stripped off all his clothes, and, jumping on its back, rode into the water till it was out of its depth; then, slipping off over the crupper, he caught hold of the tail, and as often as the horse turned round the man frightened it back by splashing water in its face. As soon as the horse touched the bottom on the other side, the man pulled himself on, and was firmly seated, bridle in hand, before the horse gained the bank. A naked man on a naked horse is a fine spectacle; I had no idea how well the two animals suited each other. The tail of a horse is a very useful appendage: I have passed a river in a boat with four people in it, which was ferried across in the same way as the Gaucho. If a man and horse have to cross a broad river, the

A NAKED MAN ON A NAKED HORSE. (ANCIENT GREEK HORSE-RACE.)

best plan is for the man to catch hold of the pommel or mane, and help himself with the other arm.

We were delayed crossing the Rio Colorado by some immense troops of mares, which were swimming the river in order to follow a division of troops into the interior. A more ludicrous spectacle I never beheld than the hundreds and hundreds of heads, all directed one way, with pointed ears and distended nostrils, appearing just above the water, like a great shoal of some amphibious animal. Mares' flesh is the only food which the soldiers have when on an expedition. This gives them a great facility of movement, for the distance to which horses can be driven over these plains is quite surprising. I have been assured that an unloaded horse can travel a hundred miles a day for many days successively.

At an *estancia* (grazing farm) near Las Vacas large numbers of mares are weekly slaughtered for the sake of their hides, although worth only five paper dollars apiece. It seems at first strange that it can answer to kill mares for such a trifle; but as it is thought ridiculous in this country ever to break in or ride a mare, they are of no value except for breeding. The only thing for which I ever saw mares used was to tread out wheat from the ear; for which purpose they were driven round a circular enclosure, where the wheat-sheaves were strewed.

It is a marvellous fact that in South America a native horse should have lived and disappeared, to be succeeded in after-ages by the countless herds descended from the few introduced with the Spanish colonists! As the remains of elephants, mastodons, horses, and hollow-horned ruminants are found on both sides of Behring's Straits and on the plains of Siberia, we are led to look to the north-western side of North America as the former point of communication between the Old and the so-called New World. And as so many species, both living and extinct, of these same genera

THRESHING CORN WITH HORSES IN ARMENIA.

inhabit and have inhabited the Old World, it seems most probable that the North American elephants, mastodons,

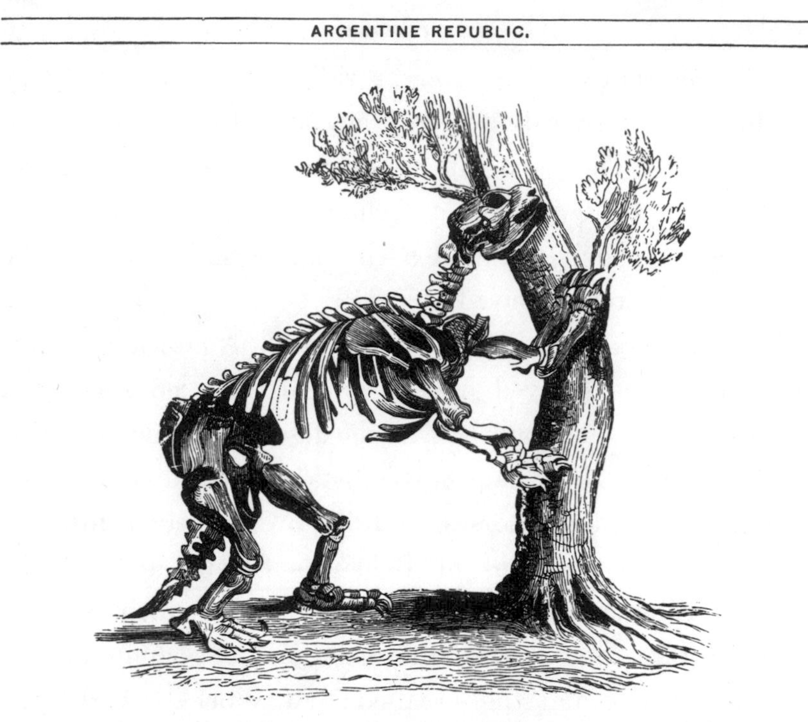

FOSSIL REMAINS OF A MEGATHERIUM.

horses, and hollow-horned ruminants migrated, on land since submerged near Behring's Straits, from Siberia into North America, and thence, on land since submerged in the West

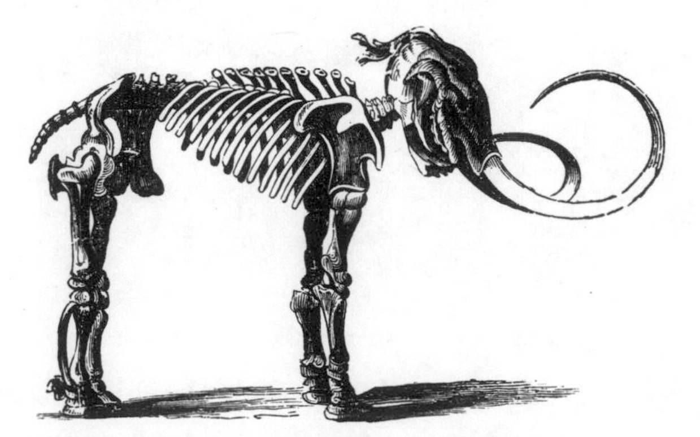

FOSSIL REMAINS OF AN ELEPHANT.

Indies, into South America, where for a time they mingled with the forms characteristic of that southern continent, and have since become extinct.

The horse was first landed at Buenos Ayres in 1537, and the colony being then for a time deserted, the horse ran wild. In 1580, only forty-three years afterward, we hear of them at the Strait of Magellan!

THE MULE.

When about half-way up the Portillo Pass, we met a large party with seventy loaded mules. It was interesting to hear the wild cries of the muleteers, and to watch the long descending string of the animals; they appeared so diminutive, there being nothing but the bleak mountains with which they could be compared. The *madrina* (or godmother) is a most important personage: she is an old, steady mare, with a little bell round her neck; and wherever she goes, the mules, like good children, follow her. The affection of these animals for their madrinas saves infinite trouble. If several large troops are turned into one field to graze, in the morning the muleteers have only to lead the madrinas a little apart, and tinkle their bells; and, although there may be two or three hundred together, each mule immediately knows the bell of its own madrina, and comes to her. It is nearly impossible to lose an old mule; for if detained for several hours by force, she will, by the power of smell, like a dog, track out her companions (or rather the madrina, for, according to the muleteer, she is the chief object of affection. I believe I am right, however, in saying that any animal with a bell will serve as a madrina). In a troop, each animal carries, on a level road, a cargo weighing four hundred and sixteen pounds, but in a mountainous country one hundred pounds less; yet with what delicate, slim limbs, without any proportional bulk of muscle, these animals support so great a burden! The mule always appears to me a most surprising animal. That the offspring of the horse and the ass should possess more reason, memory, obstinacy, social affection, powers of muscular endurance, and length of life, than either of its parents, seems to indicate that art has here outdone nature.

THE OX.

THE chief trouble with an *estancia* (grazing farm) is driving the cattle twice a week to a central spot, in order to make them tame and to count them. This latter operation would be thought difficult where there are ten or fifteen thousand head together. It is managed on the principle that the cattle invariably divide themselves into little troops (*tropillas*) of from forty to a hundred. Each troop is recognized by a few peculiarly marked animals, and its number is known; so that, one being lost out of ten thousand, it is perceived by its absence from one of the tropillas. During a stormy night the cattle all mingle together, but the next morning the tropillas separate as before; so that each animal must know its fellow out of ten thousand others.

GAUCHOS BRANDING CATTLE ON AN ESTANCIA.

THE DOG.

WHEN riding, it is a common thing to meet a large flock of sheep guarded by one or two dogs, at the distance of some miles from any house or man. I often wondered how so firm a friendship had been established. The method of education consists in separating the puppy, while very young, from its mother, and in accustoming it to its future companions. A ewe is held three or four times a day for

SHEPHERD-DOG.

the little thing to suck, and a nest of wool is made for it in the sheep-pen; at no time is it allowed to associate with other dogs, or with the children of the family. From this education, it has no wish to leave the flock; and just as another dog will defend its master, man, so will these the sheep. It is amusing to observe, when approaching a flock, how the dog immediately advances barking, and the sheep all close in his rear, as if round the oldest ram. These dogs are also easily taught to bring home the flock at a certain hour in the evening. Their most troublesome fault, when young, is their desire of playing with the sheep; for in their sport they sometimes gallop the poor things most unmercifully.

The shepherd-dog comes to the house every day for some meat, and as soon as it is given him he skulks away, as if ashamed of himself. On these occasions the house-dogs are very tyrannical, and the least of them will attack and pursue the stranger. The minute, however, the latter has reached the flock, he turns round and begins to bark, and then all the house-dogs take very quickly to their heels. In a similar manner, a whole pack of the hungry wild dogs will scarcely ever venture to attack a flock guarded by even one of these faithful shepherds. In this case the shepherd-dog seems to regard the sheep as its fellow-brethren, and thus gains confidence; and the wild dogs, though knowing that the individual sheep are not dogs, but are good to eat, yet, when seeing them in a flock with a shepherd-dog at their head, partly consent to regard them as he does.

MONKEY WITH PREHENSILE TAIL.

THE MONKEY.

During my stay at Rio de Janeiro I resided

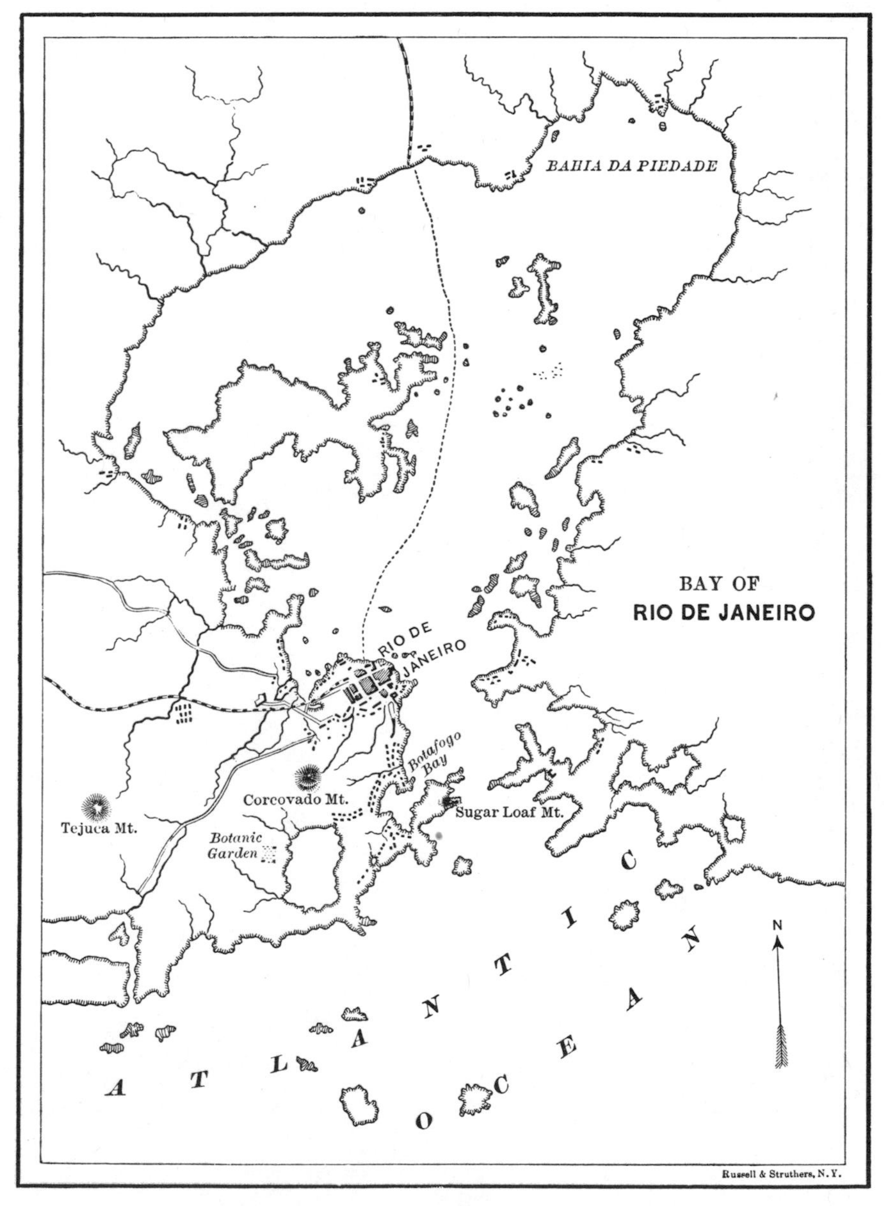
BAHIA DA PIEDADE
BAY OF
RIO DE JANEIRO
RIO DE JANEIRO
Botafogo Bay
Corcovado Mt.
Sugar Loaf Mt.
Tejuca Mt.
Botanic Garden
ATLANTIC OCEAN
N
Russell & Struthers, N.Y.

in a cottage at Botafogo Bay. An old Portuguese priest took me out to hunt with him. The sport consisted in turning into the cover a few dogs, and then patiently waiting to fire at any animal which might appear. My companion, the day before, had shot two large bearded monkeys. These animals have prehensile tails, the extremity of which, even after death, can support the whole weight of the body. One of them thus remained fast to a branch, and it was necessary to cut down a large tree to procure it. This was soon done, and down came tree and monkey with an awful crash. Our day's sport, besides the monkey, was confined to some small green parrots and a few toucans.

TOUCANS.

THE GUANACO.

The guanaco, or wild llama, is the characteristic quadruped of the plains of Patagonia; it is the South American representative of the camel of the East. It is an elegant animal in a state of nature, with a long slender neck and fine legs. It is very common over the whole of the temperate parts of the continent, as far south as the islands near Cape Horn. It generally lives in small herds of from half a dozen to thirty in each; but on the banks of the Santa Cruz we saw one herd which must have contained at least five hundred.

They are generally wild and extremely wary. The sportsman frequently receives the first notice of their pres-

THE GUANACO.

ence by hearing from a long distance their peculiar shrill neighing note of alarm. If he then looks attentively, he will probably see the herd standing in a line on the side of some distant hill. On approaching nearer, a few more squeals are given, and off they set at an apparently slow, but really quick canter, along some narrow beaten track to a neighboring hill. If, however, by chance he abruptly meets a single animal, or several together, they will generally stand motionless and intently gaze at him; then perhaps move on a few yards, turn round, and look again. What is the cause of this difference in their shyness? Do they mistake a man in the distance for their chief enemy, the puma? or does curiosity overcome their timidity? That they are curious is certain; for if a person lies on the ground, and plays strange antics, such as throwing up his feet in the air, they will almost always approach by degrees to examine him. It was a trick repeatedly practised by our sportsmen with success, and it had, moreover, the advantage of allowing several shots to be fired, which were all taken as parts of the performance. On the mountains of Tierra del Fuego I have more than once seen a guanaco, on being approached, not only neigh and squeal, but prance and leap about in the most ridiculous manner, apparently in defiance, as a challenge. These animals are very easily tamed, and I have seen some thus kept in Patagonia near a house, though not under any restraint. They are in this state very bold, and readily attack a man by striking him behind with both knees. The wild guanacos, however, have no idea of defence; even a single dog will secure one of these large animals till the huntsman can come up. In many of their habits they are like sheep in a flock. Thus, when they see men approaching in several directions on horseback, they soon become bewildered, and know not which way to run. This greatly favors the Indian mode of hunting, for they are thus easily driven to a central point and surrounded.

The guanacos readily take to the water; several times

at Port Valdes they were seen swimming from island to island. Byron, in his voyage, says he saw them drinking salt water. Some of our officers likewise saw a herd apparently drinking the briny fluid from a *salina* (salt-marsh) near Cape Blanco. I imagine that, in several parts of the country, if they do not drink salt water they drink none at all. In the middle of the day they frequently roll in the dust, in saucer-shaped hollows. Herds sometimes seem to set out on exploring parties. At Bahia Blanca, where, within thirty miles of the coast, these animals are extremely infrequent, I one day saw the track of thirty or forty, which had come in a direct line to a muddy salt-water creek. They then must have perceived that they were approaching the sea, for they had wheeled with the regularity of cavalry, and had returned back in as straight a line as they had advanced. The guanacos, like sheep, always follow the same line.

The puma, with the condor and other carrion-hawks in its train, follows and preys upon these animals. On the banks of the Santa Cruz the footsteps of the puma were to be seen almost everywhere; and the remains of several guanacos, with their necks dislocated and bones broken, showed how they had met their death.

THE PUMA.

The puma, or South American lion (*Felis concolor*), is not uncommon in Chile. This animal has a wide geographical range, being found from the equatorial forests, throughout the deserts of Patagonia, as far south as the damp and cold latitudes (fifty-three to fifty-four degrees) of Tierra del Fuego. I have seen its footsteps in the cordillera of Central Chile, at an elevation of at least ten thousand feet. In La Plata the puma preys chiefly on deer, ostriches, bizcachas, and other small quadrupeds; it there seldom attacks cattle or horses, and most rarely man. In Chile, however, it destroys many young horses and cattle, owing probably to the scarcity of other quadrupeds. I heard, likewise, of two men and a woman who had been thus killed. It is said that the puma always kills its prey by springing on the shoulders, and then drawing back the head with one of its paws until the vertebræ break. The puma, after eating its fill, covers the carcass with many large bushes, and lies down to watch it. This habit is often the cause of its being discovered; for the condors, wheeling in the air, every now and then descend to share in the feast, and, being angrily driven away, rise all together on the wing. The Chilean then knows there is a lion watching his prey; the word is given, and men and dogs hurry to the chase.

THE PUMA.

The flesh of the puma is in great esteem, resembling veal not a little both in color, taste, and flavor.

THE JAGUAR.

THE wooded banks of the great rivers appear to be the favorite haunts of the jaguar; but south of the Plata, I was told they frequented the reeds bordering lakes: wherever they are, they seem to require water. Their common prey is the capibara, or water-hog, so that it is generally said, where capibaras are numerous there is little danger from the jaguar. Falconer states that near the southern side of the mouth of the Plata there are many jaguars, and that they chiefly live on fish. This account I have heard repeated. On the Parana they have killed many wood-cutters, and have even entered vessels at night. When the floods drive these animals from the islands they are most dangerous. I was told that, a few years since, a very large one found its way into a church at Santa Fé: two priests, entering one after the other, were killed, and a third, who came to see what was the matter, escaped with difficulty. The beast was destroyed by being shot from a corner of the building which was unroofed.

THE JAGUAR.

THE CAPIBARA.

They commit, also, at these times, great ravages among cattle and horses. It is said that they kill their prey by breaking their necks. If driven from the carcass, they seldom return to it. The jaguar is a noisy animal, roaring much by night, and especially before bad weather.

One day, when hunting on the banks of the Uruguay, I was shown certain trees to which these animals constantly resort, for the purpose, as it is said, of sharpening their claws. I saw three well-known trees; in front, the bark was worn smooth, as if by the breast of the animal, and on each side there were deep scratches, or rather grooves, nearly a yard in length. The scars were of different ages. A common mode of finding out whether a jaguar is in the neighborhood, is to examine one of these trees. I imagine this habit of the jaguar is exactly similar to one which may any day be seen in the common cat, as with outstretched legs and uncovered claws it scrapes the leg of a chair; and I have heard of young fruit-trees in an orchard in England having been thus much injured. Some such habit must also be common to the puma, for on the bare, hard soil of Patagonia, I have frequently seen scores so deep that no other animal could have made them. The object of this practice is, I believe, to tear off the ragged points of their claws, and not, as the Gauchos think, to sharpen them. The jaguar is killed, without much difficulty, by the aid of dogs baying and driving him up a tree, where he is despatched with bullets.

The Gauchos differ in their opinion whether the jaguar is good eating, but are unanimous in saying that puma is excellent.

THE BIZCACHA.

THE bizcacha of the pampas (South American prairies) somewhat resembles the large rabbit, but with bigger gnawing teeth and a long tail. It is a curious circumstance in its geographical distribution that it has never been seen, fortunately for the inhabitants of Banda Oriental, to the eastward of the River Uruguay; yet in this province there are plains which appear admirably adapted to its habits. The Uruguay has formed an insuperable obstacle to its migration, although the broader barrier of the Parana has been passed, and the bizcacha is common in Entre Rios, the province between these two great rivers. Near Buenos Ayres these animals are exceedingly common. Their favorite resort appears to be those parts of the plain which, during one half of the year, are covered with giant thistles in place of all other plants. The Gauchos declare that it lives on roots—which, from the great strength of its gnawing-teeth, and the kind of places frequented by it, seems probable. In the evening the bizcachas come out in numbers, and quietly sit at the mouths of their burrows on their haunches. At such times they are very tame. They run very awkwardly, and, when running out of danger, from their uplifted tails and short front legs, much resemble great rats. Their flesh, when cooked, is very white and good, but it is seldom used.

The bizcacha has one very singular habit, namely, dragging every hard object to the mouth of its burrow: around each group of holes many bones of cattle, stones, thistle-stalks, hard lumps of earth, dry dung, etc., are collected into an irregular heap, which frequently amounts to as much as a wheelbarrow would contain. I was told, and can believe it, that a gentleman, when riding on a dark night, dropped his watch; he returned in the morning, and by searching

THE AUSTRALIAN BOWER BIRD.

the neighborhood of every bizcacha hole on the line of road, he soon found it, as he expected. This habit of picking up whatever may be lying on the ground anywhere near its habitation, must cost much trouble. For what purpose it is done I am quite unable to guess: it cannot be for defence, because the rubbish is chiefly placed above the mouth of the burrow, which enters the ground at a very small slope. No doubt there must be some good reason, but the inhabitants of the country are quite ignorant of it. The only fact which I know like it is the habit of an extraordinary Australian bird (the *Calodera maculata*), which makes an elegant vaulted passage of twigs for playing in, and which collects near the spot land and sea shells, bones, and the feathers of birds, especially brightly-colored ones. Mr. Gould tells me that the natives, when they lose any hard object, search these playing passages; and he has known a tobacco-pipe thus recovered.

THE SEAL.

I ACCOMPANIED the captain of the *Beagle* in a boat to the head of a deep creek in the Chonos Archipelago. On the way the number of seals that we saw was quite astonishing: every bit of flat rock, and parts of the beach, were covered with them. They appeared to be of a loving disposition, and lay huddled together, fast asleep, like so many pigs; but even pigs would have been ashamed of their dirt, and of the foul smell which came from them. Each herd was watched by the patient but ill-boding eyes of the turkey-buzzard. This disgusting bird, with its bald scarlet head, formed to wallow in putridity, is very common on the west coast of South America, and their attendance on the seals shows on what they rely for their food. We found the water (probably only that of the surface) nearly fresh:

THE SEAL.

this was caused by the number of torrents which, in the form of cascades, came tumbling over the bold granite moun-

THE TERN. THE GULL.

tains into the sea. The fresh water attracts the fish, and these bring many terns, gulls, and two kinds of cormorant.

We saw, also, a pair of the beautiful black-necked swans, and several small sea-otters, the fur of which is held in such high estimation. In returning, we were again amused by the impetuous manner in which the heap of seals, old and young, tumbled into the water as the boat passed. They did

THE SEA-LION.

not remain long under water, but, rising, followed us with outstretched necks, expressing great wonder and curiosity.

THE WHALE.

The fact of the Beagle Channel being an arm of the sea was made plain by several huge whales spouting in different directions. On one occasion I saw two of these monsters, probably male and female, slowly swimming, one after the other, within less than a stone's throw of the shore, over which the beech-tree extended its branches. At another time, off the east coast of Tierra del Fuego, we saw a grand sight in several spermaceti whales jumping upright, quite out of the water, with the exception of their tail-fins. As they fell down sideways they splashed the water high up, and the sound re-echoed like a distant broadside.

THE PORPOISE.

On the morning of July 5th, 1832, we got under way, and stood out of the splendid harbor of Rio de Janeiro. In our passage to the Plata we saw nothing particular, excepting on one day a great shoal of porpoises, many hundreds in number. The whole sea was in places furrowed by them; and a most extraordinary spectacle was presented, as hundreds, proceeding together by jumps, in which their whole bodies were exposed, thus cut the water. When the ship was running nine knots an hour these animals could cross and recross the bows with the greatest ease, and then dash away right ahead. As soon as we entered the estuary of the Plata the weather was very unsettled. One dark night we were surrounded by numerous seals and penguins, which made such strange noises that the officer on watch reported he could hear the cattle bellowing on shore. On a second night we witnessed a splendid scene of natural fireworks; the mast-head and yard-arm ends shone with St. Elmo's light, and the form of the vane could almost be traced, as if it had been rubbed with phosphorus. The sea was so highly luminous that the tracks of the penguins were marked by a fiery wake, and the darkness of the sky was momentarily illuminated by the most vivid lightning.

THE LIZARD.

THE *Amblyrhyncus*, a remarkable kind of lizard, is confined to the Galapagos (or Turtle) archipelago. There are two species, resembling each other in general form, one being a land, and the other a water species. The latter is extremely common on all the islands throughout the group, and lives altogether on the rocky sea-beaches, being never found (at least I never saw one) even ten yards in-shore. It is a hideous-looking creature, of a dirty black color, stupid, and sluggish in its movements. The usual length of a full-grown one is about a yard, but there are some even four feet long. Their tails are flattened sideways, and all four feet are partially webbed; and they are occasionally seen some hundred yards from the shore, swimming about. Yet, strange to say, when frightened they will not enter the water. Hence, it is easy to drive these lizards down to any little point overhanging the sea, where they will sooner allow a person to catch hold of their tails than jump into the water. They do not seem to have any notion of biting; but when much frightened they squirt a drop of fluid from each nostril. Several times I threw one as far as I could into a deep pool left by the retreating tide; but it always returned in a straight line to the spot where I stood. It swam near the bottom, with a very graceful and rapid movement, and occasionally helped itself over the uneven ground

A PHOSPHORESCENT SEA.

with its feet. As soon as it arrived near the edge, but being still under water, it tried to conceal itself in the tufts of sea-weed, or it entered some crevice. As soon as it thought the danger was past, it crawled out on the dry rocks, and shuffled away as quickly as it could. I several times caught this

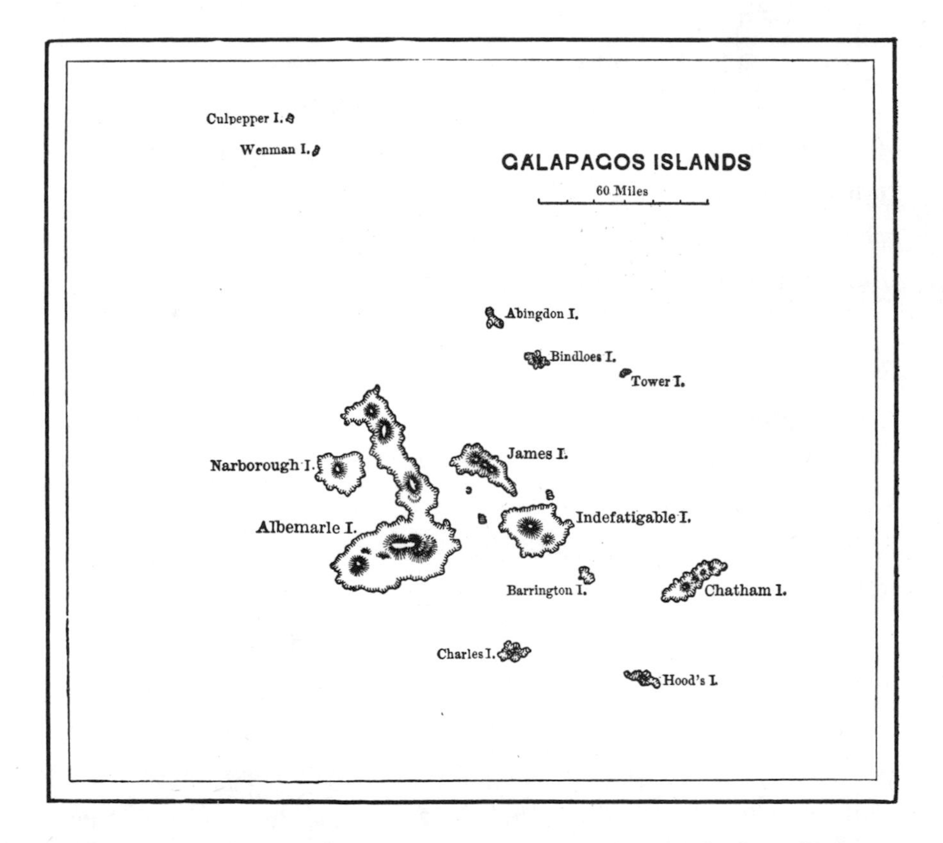

same lizard by driving it down to a point, and though having such perfect powers of diving and swimming, nothing would induce it to enter the water; and, as often as I threw it in, it returned in the manner I have just described. Perhaps this apparent stupidity may be explained by the fact that this reptile has no enemy whatever on shore, whereas at sea it must often fall a prey to the numerous sharks. Hence, probably, a fixed and hereditary instinct that the shore is its place of safety; so that whatever the danger may be, there it takes refuge.

We will now turn to the land species of *Amblyrhyncus*, with a round tail and toes without a web. Some of these lizards inhabit the high and damp parts of the islands, but they are much more numerous in the lower and barren districts near the coast. I cannot give a more forcible proof of their numbers than by stating that, when we were left at James Island, we could not for some time find a spot free from their burrows on which to pitch our single tent. Like their brothers, the sea-kind, they are ugly animals, of a yellowish orange beneath, and of a brownish-red color above. When making its burrow, this animal works by turns the opposite sides of its body. One front leg for a short time scratches up the soil and throws it toward the hind foot, which is well placed so as to heave it beyond the mouth of the hole. That side of the body being tired, the other takes up the task, and so on alternately. I watched one for a long time, till half its body was buried; I then walked up and pulled it by the tail; at this it was greatly astonished, and soon shuffled up to see what was the matter, and then stared me in the face, as much as to say, "What made you pull my tail?"

They feed by day, and do not wander far from their burrows; if frightened, they rush to them with a most awkward gait. When attentively watching any one, they curl their tails, and, raising themselves on their front legs, nod their heads up and down, and try to look very fierce; but in reality they are not at all so; if one just stamps on the ground, down go their tails, and off they shuffle as quickly as they

CACTUS GROWTH IN THE DESERTS OF UTAH.

can. I have often seen small fly-eating lizards, when watching anything, nod their heads in precisely the same manner, but I do not at all know for what purpose. If this *Amblyrhyncus* is held and plagued with a stick, it will bite it very severely; but I caught many by the tail, and they never tried to bite me. If two are placed on the ground and held together, they will fight, and bite each other till blood is drawn. The little birds know how harmless these creatures are: I have seen one of the thick-billed finches picking at one end of a piece of cactus while a lizard was eating at the other end; and afterward the little bird, with the utmost indifference, hopped on the back of the reptile. I opened the stomachs of several, and found them full of vegetable fibres and leaves of different trees, especially of an acacia. To obtain the acacia-leaves they crawl up the low, stunted trees; and it is not uncommon to see a pair quietly browsing, while seated on a branch several feet above the ground.

THE TORTOISE.

In the woods on Charles Island there are many wild pigs and goats, but the chief article of animal food is supplied by the tortoises. Their numbers have, of course, been greatly reduced, but the people yet count on two days' hunting giving them food for the rest of the week. It is said that formerly single vessels have taken away as many as seven hundred, and that the ship's company of a frigate some years since brought down, in one day, two hundred tortoises to the beach. Some grow to an immense size: Mr. Lawson, an Englishman, and vice-governor of the colony, told us that he had seen several so large that it required six or eight men to lift them from the ground, and that some had yielded as much as two hundred pounds of meat. The old males are the largest, the females rarely growing to so great a size: the male can readily be distinguished from the female by the greater length of its tail. The tortoises which live on those islands where there is no water, or in the lower and dry parts of the other islands, feed chiefly on the juicy cactus. They are very fond of water, drinking large quantities, and wallowing in the mud. The larger islands alone have springs, and these are always situated toward the central parts, and at a considerable height. The tortoises, therefore, which inhabit the lower districts, are obliged, when thirsty, to travel from a long distance. Hence, broad and well-beaten paths branch off in every direction from the wells down to the sea-coast; and the Spaniards, by following them up, first discovered the watering-places. When I landed at Chatham Island I could not imagine what animal travelled so methodically along well-chosen tracks. Near the springs it was a curious spectacle to behold many of these huge creatures—one set eagerly travelling onward with outstretched necks, and another set returning, after having drunk their fill. When the tortoise arrives at the spring he buries his head in the water above his eyes, and greedily swallows great mouthfuls, at the rate of about ten in a minute. The inhabitants say each animal

THE TORTOISE.

stays three or four days in the neighborhood of the water, and then returns to the lower country; but they differed as to the frequency of these visits, which probably depends on the nature of the food on which the animal has lived. It is, however, certain that tortoises can subsist even on those islands where there is no other water than what falls during a few rainy days in the year. I believe it is well ascertained that the bladder of the frog acts as a reservoir for the moisture necessary to its existence: such seems to be the case with the tortoise.

The tortoises, when purposely moving toward any point, travel by night and day, and arrive at their journey's end much sooner than would be expected. The inhabitants, from observing marked individuals, consider that they travel a distance of about eight miles in two or three days. One large tortoise which I watched, walked at the rate of sixty yards in ten minutes—that is, three hundred and sixty yards in the hour, or four miles a day, allowing a little time for it to eat on the road. They were at this time (October) laying their eggs. The female, where the soil is sandy, deposits them together, and covers them up with sand; but where the ground is rocky she drops them about in any hole. The young tortoises, as soon as they are hatched, fall a prey in great numbers to the carrion-feeding buzzard. The old ones seem generally to die from accidents, as from falling down precipices; at least, several of the inhabitants told me that they had never found one dead without some evident cause.

The inhabitants believe that these animals are absolutely deaf; certainly they do not overhear a person walking close behind them. I was always amused, when overtaking one of these great monsters, as it was quietly pacing along, to see how suddenly, the instant I passed, it would draw in its head and legs, and, uttering a deep hiss, fall to the ground with a heavy sound, as if struck dead. I frequently got on their backs, and then giving a few raps on the hinder part of their shells, they would rise up and walk away; but I found it very difficult to keep my balance. In order to secure the tortoises, it is not enough to turn them over like turtle, for they are often able to get on their legs again.

THE TOAD.

NEAR Bahia Blanca I found but one little toad, which was most singular from its color. If we imagine, first, that it had been steeped in the blackest ink, and then, when dry, allowed to crawl over a board freshly painted with the brightest vermilion, so as to color the soles of its feet and parts of its stomach, a good idea of its appearance will be gained. Instead of going about by night, as other toads do, and living in damp and dark recesses, it crawls during the heat of the day about the dry sand-hillocks and arid plains, where not a single drop of water can be found. It must necessarily depend on the dew for its moisture; and this, probably, is absorbed by the skin. At Maldonado I found one in a situation nearly as dry as at Bahia Blanca, and, thinking to give it a great treat, carried it to a pool of water; not only was the little animal unable to swim, but, I think, without help it would soon have been drowned.

THE CUTTLE-FISH.

I WAS much interested, on several occasions, at the Cape de Verd Islands, by watching the habits of an *Octopus*, or cuttle-fish. Although common in the pools of water left by the retiring tide, these animals were not easily caught. By means of their long arms and suckers they could drag their bodies into very narrow crevices; and, when thus fixed, it required great force to remove them. At other times they darted tail first, with the rapidity of an arrow, from one side of the pool to the other, at the same instant discoloring the water with a dark chestnut-brown ink. These animals also escape detection by a very extraordinary, chameleon-like power of changing their color. They appear to vary their tints according to the nature of the ground over which they pass: when in deep water their general shade was brownish purple, but when placed on the land, or in shallow water, this dark tint changed into one of a yellowish green. I was much amused by the various arts to escape detection used by one individual, which seemed fully aware that I was watching it. Remaining for a time motionless, it would then stealthily advance an inch or two, like a cat after a mouse,

THE CUTTLE-FISH.

sometimes changing its color; it thus proceeded till, having gained a deeper part, it darted away, leaving a dusky train of ink to hide the hole into which it had crawled. While looking for marine animals, with my head about two feet above the rocky shore, I was more than once saluted by a jet of water, accompanied by a slight grating noise. At first I could not think what it was, but afterward I found out that it was this cuttle-fish, which, though concealed in a hole, thus often led me to its discovery. From the difficulty which these animals have in carrying their heads, they cannot crawl with ease when placed on the ground.

THE CORMORANT—THE PENGUIN.

One day, in the Falkland islands, I observed a cormorant playing with a fish which it had caught. Eight times successively the bird let its prey go, then dived after it, and although in deep water, brought it each time to the surface. In the Zoölogical Gardens I have seen the otter treat a fish in the same manner, much as a cat does a mouse: I do not know of any other instance where Dame Nature seems so intentionally cruel. Another day, having placed myself between a penguin (*Aptenodytes demersa*) and the water,

THE CORMORANT.

I was much amused by watching its habits. It was a brave bird, and till reaching the sea it regularly fought and drove me backward. Nothing less than heavy blows would have stopped him; every inch he gained he firmly kept, standing close before me, erect and determined, while all the time rolling his head from side to side, in a very odd manner, as if he could only see distinctly out of the lower front part of each eye. This bird is commonly called the jackass-penguin, from its habit, while on shore, of throwing its head backward, and making a loud, strange noise, very like the braying of an ass; but while at sea, and undisturbed, its note is very deep and solemn, and is often heard in the night-time. In diving, its little wings are used as fins; but on the land, as front legs. When crawling, on four legs as it were, through the tussocks or on the side of a grassy cliff, it moves so very quickly that it might easily be mistaken for a quadruped. When at sea and fishing, it comes to the surface for the purpose of breathing with such a spring, and dives again so instantaneously, that I defy any one at first sight to be sure that it was not a fish leaping for sport.

THE CONDOR.

This day (April 27th, 1834) I shot a condor. It measured, from tip to tip of the wings, eight and a half feet, and from beak to tail, four feet. This bird is known to have a wide geographical range, being found on the west coast of South America, from the Strait of Magellan along the Cordillera as far as eight degrees north of the equator. A line of cliff near the mouth of the Santa Cruz is frequented by these birds; and about eighty miles up the river, where the sides of the valley are formed by steep basaltic precipices, the condor reappears. From these facts it seems that the condors require perpendicular cliffs. In Chile they haunt, during the greater part of the year, the lower country, near the shores of the Pacific, and at night several roost together in one tree; but in the early part of the summer they retire to the most inaccessible parts of the inner Cordillera, there to breed in peace. I was told by the country people in Chile that the condor makes no sort of nest, but in the months of November and December lays two large white eggs on a shelf of bare rock. It is said that the young condors cannot fly for an entire year; and, long after they are able, they continue to roost by night and hunt by day with their parents. The old birds generally live in pairs; but among the inland basaltic cliffs of the Santa Cruz I found a spot where scores must usually haunt. On coming suddenly to the brow of the precipice, it was a grand spectacle to see between twenty and thirty of these great birds start heavily from their resting-place and wheel

THE CONDOR.

away in majestic circles. Having gorged themselves with carrion on the plains below, they retire to these favorite ledges to digest their food. In this part of the country they live altogether on the guanacos which have died a natural death, or, as more commonly happens, have been killed by the pumas. I believe, from what I saw in Patagonia, that they do not, on ordinary occasions, extend their daily excursions to any great distance from their regular sleeping-places.

The condors may oftentimes be seen at a great height, soaring over a certain spot in the most graceful circles. On some occasions I am sure that they do this only for pleasure; but on others, the Chileno countryman tells you that they are watching a dying animal, or the puma devouring its prey. If the condors glide down, and then suddenly all rise together, the Chileno knows that it is the puma, which, watching the carcass, has sprung out to drive away the robbers. Besides feeding on carrion, the condors frequently attack young goats and lambs; and the shepherd-dogs are trained, whenever the birds pass over, to run out, and, looking upward, to bark violently. The Chilenos destroy and catch numbers. Two methods are used: one is to place a carcass on a level piece of ground within an enclosure of sticks, having an opening, and, when the condors are gorged, to gallop up on horseback to the entrance, and thus enclose them; for when this bird has not space to run, it cannot give its body sufficient momentum to rise from the ground. The second method is to mark the trees in which, frequently to the number of five or six together, they roost, and then at night to climb up and noose them. They are such heavy sleepers, as I have myself witnessed, that this is not a difficult task. At Valparaiso I have seen a living condor sold for sixpence, but the common price is eight or ten shillings. In a garden, at the same place, between twenty and thirty were kept alive.

When an animal is killed in the country, it is well known that the condors, like other carrion-vultures, soon learn of it, and congregate in a manner not yet explained. In most cases, too, the birds have discovered their prey and picked the skeleton clean before the flesh is in the least degree tainted. Remembering the experiments of Mr. Audubon on the little smelling powers of carrion-hawks, I tried, in the above-mentioned garden, the following experiment: the condors were tied, each by a rope, in a long row at the bottom of a wall, and having folded up a piece of meat in white paper, I walked backward and forward, carrying it in my hand at the distance of about three yards from them, but no notice whatever was taken. I then threw it on the ground, within one yard of an old male bird; he looked at it for a moment with attention, but then regarded it no more. With a stick I pushed it closer and closer, until at last he touched it with his beak; the paper was then instantly torn off with fury, and at the same moment every bird in the long row began struggling and flapping its wings. Under the same circumstances it would have been quite impossible to have deceived a dog.

Often, when lying down to rest on the open plains, on looking upward I have seen carrion-hawks sailing through the air at a great height. Where the country is level, I do not believe a space of the heavens of more than fifteen degrees above the horizon is commonly viewed with any attention by a person, either walking or on horseback. If such be the case, and the vulture is on the wing at a height of between three and four thousand feet, before it could come within the range of vision its distance in a straight line from the beholder's eye would be rather more than two British miles. Might it not thus readily be overlooked? When an animal is killed by the sportsman in a lonely valley, may he not all the while be watched from above by the sharp-sighted bird? And will not the manner of its descent proclaim throughout the district to the whole family of carrion-feeders that their prey is at hand?

When the condors are wheeling in a flock round and round any spot, their flight is beautiful. Except when rising from the ground, I do not recollect ever having seen one of these birds flap its wings. Near Lima, I watched several for nearly half an hour, without once taking off my eyes: they moved in large curves, sweeping in circles, descending and ascending without giving a single flap. As they glided close over my head, I intently watched from an oblique position the outlines of the separate and great terminal feathers of each wing; and these separate feathers, if there had been the least vibratory movement, would have appeared as if blended together; but they were seen distinct against the blue sky. The head and neck were moved frequently, and apparently with great force; and the outstretched wings seemed to form the fulcrum on which the movements of the neck, body, and tail acted. If the bird wished to descend, the wings were for a moment collapsed; and when again expanded with an altered inclination, the momentum gained by the rapid descent seemed to urge the bird upward with the even and steady movement of a paper kite. It is truly wonderful and beautiful to see so great a bird, hour after hour, without any apparent exertion, wheeling and gliding over mountain and river.

THE OSTRICH.

On the fine plains of turf in Banda Oriental we saw many ostriches (*Struthio rhea*). Some of the flocks contained as many as twenty or thirty birds. These, when standing on any little height and seen against the clear sky, presented a very noble appearance. I never met with such tame ostriches in any other part of the country: it was easy to gallop up within a short distance of them; but then, expanding their wings, they made all sail before the wind, and soon left the horse astern.

The ostrich is the largest of the birds which are common on the wild plains of Northern Patagonia. It lives on vegetable matter, such as roots and grass; but at Bahia Blanca I have repeatedly seen three or four come down at low water to the extensive mud-banks, which are then dry, for the sake, as the Gauchos say, of feeding on small fish. Although the ostrich in its habits is so shy, wary, and solitary, and although so fleet in its pace, it is caught without much difficulty by the Indian or Gaucho armed with the *bolas* (two round stones, covered with leather, and united by a thin plaited thong about eight feet long). When several horsemen appear in a semicircle, the bird becomes confounded, and does not know which way to escape. They generally prefer running against the wind, yet at the first start they expand their wings, and like a vessel make all sail. On one fine hot day I saw several ostriches enter a bed of tall rushes, where they squatted concealed till quite closely approached. It is not generally known that ostriches readily take to the water. Mr. King informs me that at the Bay of San Blas, and at Port Valdes, in Patagonia, he saw these birds swimming several times from island to island. They ran into the water, both when driven down to a point, and likewise of their own accord when not frightened; the distance crossed was about two hundred yards.

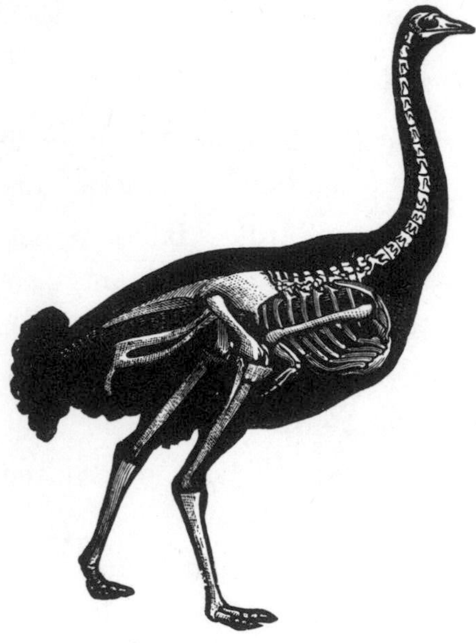
SKELETON OF AN OSTRICH.

When swimming, very little of their bodies appears above water; their necks are stretched a little forward, and their progress is slow. On two occasions I saw some ostriches swimming across the Santa Cruz River, where its course was about four hundred yards wide and the stream rapid. Captain Sturt, when descending the Murrumbidgee, in Australia, saw two emus in the act of swimming.

The inhabitants of the country can readily tell, even at a distance, the cock bird from the hen. The former is larger, and darker colored, and has a bigger head. The ostrich (I believe, the cock) utters a singular deep-toned, hissing note; when I first heard it, standing in the midst of some sand-hillocks, I thought it was made by some wild beast, for it is a sound that one cannot tell whence it comes or from how far distant. When we were at Bahia Blanca, in the months of September and October, the eggs, in extraordinary numbers, were found all over the country. They lie either scattered and single (in which case they are never hatched, and are called by the Spaniards *huachos*), or they are collected together into a shallow excavation, which forms the nest. Out of the four nests which I saw, three contained twenty-two eggs each, and the fourth twenty-seven. Each of these is said to equal in weight eleven hen eggs; so that we obtained from this last nest as much food as two hundred and ninety-seven hen eggs would have given. The Gauchos all agree in saying that there is no reason to doubt that the male bird alone hatches the eggs, and for some time afterward accompanies the young. The cock, when on the nest, lies very close; I have myself almost ridden over one. At such times they are said to be occasionally fierce and even dangerous, and to have been known to attack a man on horseback, trying to kick and leap on him. My informer pointed out to me an old man whom he had seen much terrified by one chasing him. I observe, in Burchell's travels in South Africa, that he remarks, "Having killed a male ostrich, and the feathers being dirty, it was said by the Hottentots to be a nest bird." I understand that the male emu in the London Zoölogical Gardens takes charge of the nest: this habit, therefore, is common to the family.

THE CASARITA.

THE casarita (little housebuilder) as the Spaniards call it, from its resemblance to the casara (housebuilder or oven-bird), makes its nest at the bottom of a narrow cylindrical hole, which is said to extend horizontally to nearly six feet under ground. Several of the country people told me that when boys they had attempted to dig out the nest, but had scarcely ever succeeded in getting to the end of the passage. The bird chooses any low bank of firm sandy soil by the side of a road or stream. Here (at Bahia Blanca) the walls round the houses are built of hardened mud, and I noticed that one, which enclosed a court-yard where I lodged, was bored through by round holes in a score of places. On asking the owner the cause of this, he bitterly complained of the little casarita, several of which I afterward observed at work. It is rather curious to find how unable these birds must be to get any idea of thickness, for although they were constantly flitting over the low wall, they kept on vainly boring through it, thinking it an excellent bank for their nests. I do not doubt that each bird, as often as it came to daylight on the opposite side, was greatly surprised at the marvellous fact.

TAME BIRDS ON DESERT ISLANDS.

We found, on St. Paul's Rocks, only two kinds of birds —the booby and the noddy. The former is a species of gannet, and the latter a tern. Both are of a tame and stupid disposition, and are so unused to visitors that I could have

ST. PAUL'S ROCKS.

killed any number of them with my geological hammer. The booby lays her eggs on the bare rock; but the tern makes a very simple nest with sea-weed. By the side of many of these nests a small flying-fish was placed, which, I suppose, had been brought by the male bird for its partner. It was amusing to watch how quickly a large and active crab, which inhabits the crevices of the rocks, stole the fish from the side of the nest as soon as we had disturbed the parent birds. Sir W. Symonds, one of the few persons who have landed

THE NODDY.

here, informs me that he saw the crabs dragging even the young birds out of their nests and devouring them.

Extreme tameness is common to all the land-birds in the Galapagos Islands, namely, to the mocking-thrushes, the finches, wrens, tyrant fly-catchers, the dove, and carrion-buzzard. All of them often approached sufficiently near to be killed with a switch, and sometimes, as I myself tried, with a cap or hat. A gun is here almost superfluous; for with the muzzle I pushed a hawk off the branch of a tree. One day, while lying down, a mocking-thrush alighted on the edge of a pitcher, made of the shell of a tortoise, which I held in my hand, and began very quietly to sip the water; it allowed me to lift it from the ground while seated on the vessel. I often tried, and very nearly succeeded, in catching these birds by their legs. Formerly the birds appear to have been even tamer than at present. Cowley (in the year 1684) says that the "turtle-doves were so tame that they would often alight upon our hats and arms, so as that we could take them alive: they not fearing man until such time as some of our company did fire at them, whereby they were rendered more shy." Dampier, also, in the same year, says that a man in a morning's walk might kill six or seven dozen of these doves. At present, although certainly very tame, they do not alight on people's arms, nor do they suffer them-

FLYING-FISH.

selves to be killed in such large numbers. It is surprising that they have not become wilder, for these islands during the last hundred and fifty years have been frequently visited by buccaneers and whalers, and the sailors, wandering through the woods in search of tortoises, always take cruel delight in knocking down the little birds. In Charles Island, which had then been settled about six years, I saw a boy sitting by a well with a switch in his hand, with which he killed the doves and finches as they came to drink. He had already got a little heap of them for his dinner, and he said that he had constantly been in the habit of waiting by this well for the same purpose. It would seem that the birds of this archipelago, not having as yet learned that man is a more dangerous animal than the tortoise or the lizard (*Amblyrhyncus*), disregard him, just as in England shy birds, such as magpies, do not mind the cows and horses grazing in the fields.

HEAD OF A FLY-CATCHER.

THE TURTLE-DOVE.

The Falkland Islands offer a second instance of birds with a similar disposition. As the birds are so tame there, where foxes, hawks, and owls occur, we may infer that the absence of all beasts of prey at the Galapagos is not the cause of their tameness here. The upland geese at the Falklands show, by the precaution they take in building on the islets, that they are aware of their danger from the foxes;

"EARTH" OF THE FOX.

but this does not make them wild toward man. In the Falklands, the sportsman may sometimes kill more of the upland geese in one day than he can carry home; whereas in Tierra del Fuego, where the same species has for ages past been persecuted by the wild inhabitants, it is nearly as difficult to kill one as it is in England to shoot the common wild goose. In the time of Pernety (1763) all the birds at the Falklands appear to have been much tamer than at present, and about as tame as they now are at the Galapagos. Even formerly, when all the birds were so tame, it was impossible, by Pernety's account, to kill the black-necked swan—a bird of passage, which probably brought with it the wisdom learned in foreign countries.

WILD GOOSE.

From these several facts we may, I think, conclude that there is no way of accounting for the wildness of birds toward man except as an inherited habit. Comparatively few young birds, in any one year, have been injured by man in England, yet almost all, even nestlings, are afraid of him. On the other hand, many individual birds, both at the Galapagos and at the Falklands, have been pursued and injured by

THE OWL.

man, but yet have not learned a wholesome dread of him. From these facts, too, we may guess what havoc the introduction of any new beast of prey must cause in a country before the instincts of the native inhabitants have become adapted to the stranger's craft or power.

THE GRASSHOPPER.

THE most remarkable instance I have known of an insect being caught far from the land, was that of a large grasshopper (*Acrydium*), which flew on board when the *Beagle* was to windward of the Cape de Verd Islands, and when the nearest point of land not directly opposed to the trade-wind was Cape Blanco, on the coast of Africa, three hundred and seventy miles distant.

THE GRASSHOPPER.

THE LOCUST.

SHORTLY before we arrived at Luxan (province of Mendoza, La Plata) we observed to the south a ragged cloud, of a dark reddish-brown color. At first we thought that it was smoke from some great fire on the plains; but we soon found that it was a swarm of locusts. They were flying northward; and, with the aid of a light breeze, they overtook us at a rate of ten or fifteen miles an hour. The main body filled the air from a height of twenty feet to that, as it appeared, of two or three thousand above the ground; "and the

LOCUSTS.

sound of their wings was as the sound of chariots of many horses running to battle;" or rather, I should say, like a strong breeze passing through the rigging of a ship. They were not so thick together but that they could escape a stick waved backward and forward. The poor cottagers in vain attempted, by lighting fires, by shouts, and by waving branches, to ward off the attack. When the locusts alighted they were more numerous than the leaves in the field, and the surface became reddish instead of green. Locusts are not an uncommon pest in this country; already, during this season, several smaller swarms had come up from the south, where, as apparently in all other parts of the world, they are bred in the deserts.

THE ANT.

A SMALL dark-colored ant sometimes migrates in great numbers. One day, at Bahia, my attention was drawn by observing many spiders, cockroaches, and other insects, and some lizards, rushing in the greatest agitation across a bare

AN ARMY OF ANTS.

piece of ground. A little way behind, every stalk and leaf was blackened by a small ant. The swarm having crossed the bare space, divided itself and descended an old wall. By this means many insects were fairly enclosed; and the efforts which the poor little creatures made to extricate themselves from such a death were wonderful. When the ants came to the road they changed their course, and in narrow files reascended the wall. When I placed a small stone so as to intercept one of the lines, the whole body attacked it, and then immediately retired. Shortly afterward another body came to the charge, and again having failed to make any impression, this line of march was entirely given up. By going an inch round the file might have avoided the stone, and this doubtless would have happened if it had been there in the beginning; but having been attacked, the lion-hearted little warriors scorned the idea of yielding.

THE WASP.

I WAS much interested one day by watching, in the neighborhood of Rio, a deadly contest between a *Pepsis* and a large spider of the genus *Lycosa.* The wasp made a sudden dash at its prey, and then flew away: the spider was evidently wounded, for, trying to escape, it rolled down a little slope, but had still strength enough to crawl into a thick tuft of grass. The wasp soon returned, and seemed surprised at not finding its victim at once. It then commenced as regular a hunt as ever hound did after fox; making short half-circuits, and all the time rapidly vibrating its wings and antennæ. The spider, though well hidden, was soon discovered; and the wasp, evidently still afraid of its jaws, inflicted two stings on the under side of its thorax. At last, carefully examining with its antennæ the now motionless spider, it proceeded to drag away the body. But I stopped both tyrant and prey.

WASP AND SPIDER.

THE SPIDER.

It is well known that most British spiders, when a large insect is caught in their webs, try to cut the lines and set free their prey, to save their nets from being entirely spoiled. I once, however, saw, in a hot-house in Shropshire, a large female wasp caught in the irregular web of a very small spider, and this spider, instead of cutting the web, most perseveringly continued to entangle the body, and especially the wings, of its prey. The wasp at first aimed in vain repeated thrusts with its sting at its little antagonist. Pitying the wasp, after allowing it to struggle for more than an hour, I killed it and put it back into the web. The spider soon returned; and an hour afterward I was much surprised to find it with its jaws buried in the opening through which the sting is thrust out by the living wasp. I drove the spider away two or three times, but for the

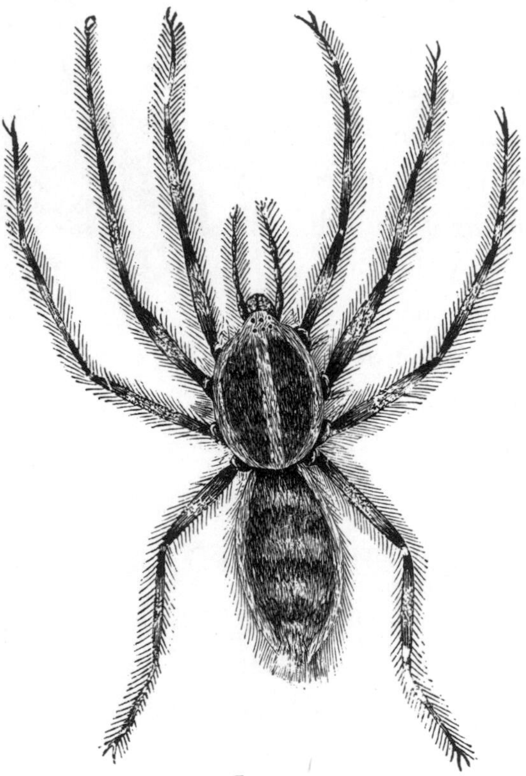

THE SPIDER (*Lycosa gyrophora*).

next twenty-four hours I always found it again sucking at the same place. It became much swollen by the juices of its prey, which was many times larger than itself.

THE CRAB.

THERE is found on Keeling Island a crab which lives on the cocoa-nuts: it is very common on all parts of the

THE ROBBER-CRAB.

dry land, and grows to a monstrous size. The front pair of legs end in very strong and heavy pincers, and the last pair are fitted with others weaker and much narrower. It would at first be thought quite impossible for a crab to open a strong cocoa-nut covered with the husk; but Mr. Liesk assures me that he has repeatedly seen this done. The crab begins by tearing the husk, fibre by fibre, and always from that end under which the three eye-holes are situated; when this is completed, the crab commences hammering with its heavy claws on one of the eye-holes till an opening is made. Then, turning round its body, by the aid of its narrow pincers behind it draws out the white meat. I think this is as curious a case of instinct as I ever heard of, and likewise of adaptation in structure between two objects apparently so unconnected by nature as a crab and a cocoa-nut tree. These crabs inhabit deep burrows, which they hollow out beneath the roots of trees, and where they accumulate surprising quantities of the picked fibres of the cocoa-nut husk, on which they rest as on a bed. They are very good to eat; moreover, under the tail of the larger ones there is a great mass of fat, which, when melted, sometimes yields as much as a quart bottle full of clear oil. To show the wonderful strength of the front pair of pincers, I may mention that Captain Moresby shut one up in a strong tin box, which had held biscuits, the lid being secured with wire; but the crab turned down the edges and escaped. In turning down the edges it actually punched many small holes quite through the tin.

II.

MAN.

THE SAVAGE.

SOUTH AMERICA.

PERHAPS nothing is more certain to create astonishment than the first sight, in his native haunt, of a barbarian —of man in his lowest and most savage state. One's mind hurries back over past centuries, and then asks, Could our forefathers have been men like these?—men whose very

THE LION IN HIS DESERT.

signs and expressions are less intelligible to us than those of the domesticated animals; men who do not possess the instinct of those animals, nor yet appear to boast of human reason, or at least of arts which result from that reason. I do not believe it is possible to describe or paint the difference between savage and civilized man. It is the difference between a wild and a tame animal (only greater, because in man there is a greater power of improvement); and part of the interest in beholding a savage is the same which would make every one desire to see the lion in his desert, the tiger tearing his prey in the jungle, or the rhinoceros wandering over the wild plains of Africa.

THE RHINOCEROS.

THE FUEGIAN.

THE Fuegians of Good Success Bay are a very different race from the stunted, miserable wretches farther westward; and they seem closely related to the famous Patagonians of the Strait of Magellan. Their only garment consists of a mantle made of guanaco skin, with the wool outside. This they wear just thrown over their shoulders, leaving their persons as often exposed as covered. Their skin is of a dirty coppery-red color. Their chief spokesman, an old man, had a fillet of white feathers tied round his head, which partly confined his black, coarse, and entangled hair. His face was crossed by two broad bars: one, painted bright red, reached from ear to ear, and included the upper lip; the other, white like chalk, stretched above the first so that even his eyelids were thus colored. His two companions, younger and powerful men, about six feet high, were ornamented by streaks of black powder, made of charcoal. The party altogether closely resembled the devils which come on the stage in plays like "Der Freischütz."

Their very attitudes were abject, and the expression of their countenances distrustful, surprised, and startled. After we had presented them with some scarlet cloth, which they immediately tied round their necks, they became good friends. This was shown by the old man patting our breasts and making a chuckling kind of noise, as people do when feeding chickens. I walked with the old man, and this demonstration of friendship was repeated several times, ending in three hard slaps, which were given me on the breast and back at the same time. He then bared his bosom for me to return the compliment, which being done, he seemed highly pleased.

The language of these people, according to our notions, scarcely deserves to be called articulate. Captain Cook has compared it to a man clearing his throat; but certainly no European ever cleared his throat with so many hoarse, guttural and clicking sounds. They are excellent mimics: as often as we coughed, or yawned, or made any odd motion, they immediately imitated us. Some of our party began to squint and look awry; but one of the young Fuegians (whose whole face was painted black, excepting a white band across his eyes) succeeded in making far more hideous grimaces. They could repeat with perfect correctness each word in any sentence we addressed them, and they remembered such words for some time. Yet we Europeans all know how difficult it is to distinguish apart the sounds in a foreign

NORTH AMERICAN INDIAN (WINNEBAGO).

language. Which of us, for instance, could follow an American Indian through a sentence of more than three words? All savages seem to have, to an uncommon degree, this power of mimicry: I was told, almost in the same words, of the same laughable habit among the South African Kaffirs; the Australians, likewise, have long been notorious for being able to imitate and describe the gait of any man so that he may be recognized. How can this faculty be explained? Does it come from the more practised habits of perception and keener senses common to all men in a savage state, as compared with those long civilized?

The inhabitants of Tierra del Fuego, living chiefly upon shell-fish, are obliged constantly to change their place of residence; but they return at intervals to the same spots, as is

AUSTRALIAN ABORIGINES.

evident from the piles of old shells, which must often amount to many tons in weight. These heaps can be recognized at a long distance by the bright green color of certain plants which always grow on them. Among these are the wild celery and scurvy-grass, two very serviceable plants, the use of which has not been discovered by the natives. The Fuegian wigwam resembles, in size and dimensions, a hay-cock.

A SOUTH AFRICAN KAFFIR.

It consists merely of a few broken branches stuck in the ground, and very rudely thatched on one side with a few tufts of grass and rushes. The whole cannot be the work of an hour, and it is only used for a few days. On the west coast, however, the wigwams are rather better, for they are covered with seal-skins.

While going one day on shore near Wollaston Island, we pulled alongside a canoe with six Fuegians. These were the most abject and miserable creatures I anywhere beheld. On the east coast the natives, as we have seen, have guanaco cloaks, and on the west they possess seal-skins. Among these central tribes the men generally have an otter-skin, or some small scrap, about as large as a pocket-handkerchief, which is barely sufficient to cover their backs as low down as their loins. It is laced across the breast by strings, and, according as the wind blows, it is shifted from side to side. But these Fuegians in the canoe were quite naked, and even one full-grown woman was absolutely so. It was raining heavily, and the fresh water, together with the spray, trickled down her body. In another harbor, not far distant, a woman who was suckling a newly-born child came one day alongside the vessel, and remained there, out of mere curiosity, while the sleet fell and thawed on her naked bosom and on the skin of her naked baby! These poor wretches were stunted in their growth, their hideous faces bedaubed with white paint, their skins filthy and greasy, their hair entangled, their voices discordant, and their gestures violent. Viewing such men, one can hardly make one's self believe that they are fellow-creatures, and inhabitants of the same world. We often try to imagine what pleasure in life some of the lower animals can enjoy: how much more reasonably the same question may be asked concerning these barbarians! At night five or six human beings, naked, and scarcely protected from the wind and rain of this tempestuous climate, sleep on the wet ground, coiled up like animals. Whenever it is low

A FUEGIAN FEAST.

water—winter or summer, night or day—they must rise to pick shell-fish from the rocks; and the women either dive to collect sea-eggs or sit patiently in their canoes, and with a baited hair-line, without any hook, jerk out little fish. If a seal is killed, or the floating carcass of a putrid whale discovered, it is a feast; and such miserable food is assisted by a few tasteless berries and fungi.

They often suffer from famine: I heard Mr. Low, a sealing-master very well acquainted with the natives of this country, give a curious account of the state of a party of one hundred and fifty natives on the west coast, who were very thin, and in great distress. A succession of gales prevented the women from getting shell-fish on the rocks, and they could not go out in their canoes to catch seal. A small party of these men one morning set out on a four days' journey for food; on their return Low went to meet them, and found them excessively tired—each man carrying a great square piece of putrid whale's-blubber, with a hole in the middle, through which he put his head, as the Gauchos do through their *ponchos* or cloaks. As soon as the blubber was brought into a wigwam an old man cut off the slices, and, muttering over them, broiled them for a minute, and distributed them to the famished party, who, during this time, preserved a profound silence. Mr. Low believes that whenever a whale is cast on shore the natives bury large pieces of it in the sand as a resource in time of famine. The different tribes, when at war, are cannibals; and it is certainly true that, when pressed in winter by hunger, they kill and devour their old women before they kill their dogs. A boy, being asked by Mr. Low why they did this, answered: "Doggies catch otters, old women no."

Few, if any, of the natives in the Beagle Channel could ever have seen a white man; certainly nothing could exceed their astonishment at the sight of our four boats. Fires were lighted on every point (hence the name of Tierra del Fuego, or the land of fire), both to attract our attention and to spread far and wide the news. Some of the men ran for miles along the shore. I shall never forget how wild and savage one group appeared: suddenly four or five men came to the edge of an overhanging cliff; they were absolutely naked, and their long hair streamed about their faces. They held rough staves in their hands, and, springing from the ground, waved their arms round their heads, and sent forth the most hideous yells. At dinner-time we landed among a party of Fuegians. At first they were not inclined to be friendly, for, until Captain Fitz Roy pulled in ahead of the other boats, they kept their slings in their hands. We soon, however, delighted them by trifling presents, such as tying red tape round their heads. They liked our biscuit: but one of the savages touched with his finger some of the meat, preserved in tin cases, which I was eating, and feeling it soft and cold, he showed as much disgust at it as I should have done at putrid blubber. It was as easy to please as it was hard to satisfy these savages. Young and old, men and children, never ceased repeating the word "Yammerschooner," which means "give me," and pointing to almost every object, one after the other, even to the buttons on our coats. At night we slept close to the junction of Ponsonby Sound with the Beagle Channel. A small family of Fuegians, who were living in the cove, were quiet and inoffensive, and soon joined our party round a blazing fire. We were well clothed, and, though sitting close to the fire, were far from too warm; yet these naked savages, though farther off, were observed, to our great surprise, to be streaming with perspiration from such a roasting. They seemed, however, very well pleased, and all joined in the chorus of the seamen's songs; but the way in which they were always behindhand was very ludicrous.

I believe that man, in this extreme part of South America, exists in a lower state of improvement than in any other part of the world. The South Sea Islanders, of the two races inhabiting the Pacific, are comparatively civilized. The Es-

SOUTH SEA ISLANDERS.

kimo, in his underground hut, enjoys some of the comforts of life, and in his canoe, when fully equipped, shows much skill. Some of the tribes of Southern Africa, prowling about in search of roots, and living hid on the wild and parched plains, are wretched enough. The Australian, in the simplicity of the arts of life, comes nearest the Fuegian; he can,

BUSHMEN OF SOUTH AFRICA.

however, boast of his boomerang, his spear and throwing-stick; his mode of climbing trees, of tracking animals, and of hunting. But although the Australian may be superior in acquirements, it by no means follows that he is likewise superior in mental capacity. Indeed, from what I saw of the Fuegians, and from what I have read of the Australians, I should think the opposite was true.

THE PATAGONIAN.

At Cape Gregory the famous so-called *gigantic* Patagonians gave us a hearty reception. Their height appears greater than it really is, from their large guanaco mantles, their long flowing hair, and general figure: on an average their height is about six feet, with some men taller, and only a few shorter; and the women are also tall. Altogether they are certainly the tallest race that we anywhere saw. In features they strikingly resemble the more northern Indians whom I saw with Rosas, but they have a wilder and more formidable appearance: their faces were much painted with red and black, and one man was ringed and dotted with white, like a Fuegian. Captain Fitz Roy offered to take any three of them on board, and all seemed determined to be of the three: it was long before we could clear the boat. At last we got on board with our three giants, who dined with the captain and behaved quite like gentlemen, helping themselves with knives, forks, and spoons: nothing was so much relished as sugar. The tribe spend the greater part of the year here, but in summer they hunt along the foot of the Cordillera; sometimes they travel as far as the Rio Negro, seven hundred and fifty miles to the north. They are well stocked with horses, each man having, according to Mr. Low, six or seven, and all the women, and even the children, their one own horse. Mr. Low informs me that a neighboring tribe of foot-Indians is now (1834) changing into horse-Indians.

THE INDIAN OF THE PAMPAS.

We stayed two days at the Colorado, near the encampment of General Rosas. My chief amusement was watching the Indian families, as they came to buy little articles at the rancho where we stayed. It was supposed that General Rosas had about six hundred Indian allies. The men were

LENGUA INDIANS (BASIN OF THE PLATE RIVER).

a tall, fine race, yet it was afterward easy to see in the Fuegian savage the same countenance made hideous by cold, want of food, and less civilization. Among the young women, or *chinas*, some deserve to be called even beautiful. Their hair was coarse, but bright and black, and they wore it in two plaits, hanging down to the waist. They had a high color, and eyes that glistened with brilliancy. Their legs, feet, and arms were small, and elegantly formed; their ankles, and sometimes their waists, were ornamented by broad bracelets of blue beads. Nothing could be more interesting than some of the family groups. A mother with one or two daughters would often come to our rancho mounted upon the same horse. They ride like men, but with their knees tucked up higher; a habit which comes, perhaps, of their being accustomed, when travelling, to ride the loaded horses. The duty of the women is to load and unload the horses; to make the tents for the night; in short, to be, like the wives of all savages, useful slaves. The men fight, hunt, take care of the horses, and make the riding-gear. One of their chief in-door occupations is to knock two stones together till they become round, in order to make the *bolas*. With this important weapon the Indian catches his game, and also his

SOLDIERS OF GENERAL ROSAS.

horse, which roams free over the plain. In fighting, his first attempt is to throw down his enemy's horse with the *bolas*, and when entangled by the fall, to kill him with his pike (*chuzo*). If the *bolas* only catch the neck or body of an animal, they are often carried away and lost. As the making of the stones round is the labor of two days, the manufacture of the balls is a very common employment. Several of the men and women had their faces painted red, but I never saw the horizontal bands which are so common among the Fuegians. Their chief pride consists in having everything made of silver. I have seen a cacique with his spurs, stirrups, handle of his knife, and bridle, made of this metal. The headstall and reins, being of wire, were not thicker than whip-cord; and to see a fiery steed wheeling about under the command of so light a chain gave to the horsemanship a remarkable character of elegance.

The chief Indians always have one or two picked horses, which they keep ready for any urgent occasion. When the troops of General Rosas first arrived at Cholechel they found there a tribe of Indians, of whom they killed twenty or thirty. The cacique escaped in a manner which astonished every one. He sprang upon an old white horse, taking with him his little son. The horse had neither saddle nor bridle. To avoid the shots, the Indian rode in the peculiar manner of his nation, namely, with an arm round the horse's neck, and one leg only on its back. Thus hanging on one side, he was seen patting the horse's head, and talking to him. The pursuers made every effort in the chase; the commandant three times changed his horse; but all in vain. The old Indian father and his son escaped and were free. What a fine picture one can form in one's mind—the naked, bronze-like figure of the old man, with his little boy, riding like Mazeppa on the white horse, thus leaving far behind him the host of pursuers!

In a battle at the small Salinas a tribe, consisting of about one hundred and ten Indians, men, women, and children, were nearly all taken or killed. Four men ran away together. They were pursued: one was killed, and the other three were taken alive. They turned out to be messengers from a large body of Indians, united in the common cause of defence, near the Cordillera. The tribe to which they had been sent was on the point of holding a grand council; the feast of mare's flesh was ready, and the dance prepared: in the morning the messengers were to have returned to the Cordillera. They were remarkably fine men, very fair, above six feet high, and all under thirty years of age. The three survivors, of course, possessed very valuable information, and to extort this they were placed in a line. The two first, being questioned, answered, "No sé" (I do not know), and were one after the other shot. The third also said "No sé;" adding, "Fire! I am a man, and can die!" Not one syllable would they breathe to injure the united cause of their country.

During my stay at Bahia Blanca, while waiting for the *Beagle*, an account came that a small party, forming one of the *postas* on the line to Buenos Ayres, had been found all murdered. The next day three hundred men arrived from the Colorado, a large portion of whom were Indians, and passed the night here. In the morning they started for the scene of the murder, with orders to follow the *rastro* or track, even if it led them to Chile. One glance at the rastro tells these people a whole history. Supposing they examine the track of a thousand horses, they will soon guess the number of mounted ones by seeing how many have cantered; by the depth of the other impressions, whether any horses were loaded with cargoes; by the irregularity of the footsteps, how far tired; by the manner in which the food has been cooked, whether the pursued travelled in haste; by the general appearance, how long it has been since they passed. They consider a rastro ten days or a fortnight old quite recent enough to be hunted out.

In journeying from the Rio Negro to the Colorado we came in sight of a famous tree, which the Indians reverence as the altar of Walleechu. It stands on a high part of the plain, and hence is a landmark visible at a great distance. As soon as a tribe of Indians come in sight of it they offer their adorations by loud shouts. The tree itself is low, much branched, and thorny: just above the root it has a diameter of about three feet. It stands by itself, without any neighbor, and was indeed the first tree we saw; afterward we met with a few others of the same kind, but they were far from common. Being winter, the tree had no leaves, but in their place numberless threads, by which the various offerings, such as cigars, bread, meat, pieces of cloth, etc., had been hung upon it. Poor Indians, not having anything better, only pull a thread out of their ponchos and fasten it to the tree. Richer Indians are accustomed to pour spirits and *matë* (tea) into a certain hole, and likewise to smoke upward, thinking thus to afford all possible gratification to Walleechu. To complete the scene, the tree was surrounded by the bleached bones of horses which had been slaughtered as sacrifices.

All Indians, of every age and sex, make their offerings; they then think that their horses will not tire, and that they themselves shall be prosperous. The Gaucho who told me this said that, in the time of peace, he had witnessed this scene, and that he and others used to wait till the Indians had passed by, for the sake of stealing from Walleechu the offerings. The Gauchos think that the Indians consider the tree as the god himself; but it seems far more probable that they regard it as his altar.

THE NEGRO.

We determined to pass the night at one of the post-houses, a day's ride from Bahia Blanca. This *posta* was commanded by a negro lieutenant, born in Africa; and, to his credit be it said, there was not a rancho between the Colorado and Buenos Ayres in nearly such neat order as his. He had a little room for strangers, and a small corral for the horses, all made of sticks and reeds; he had also dug a ditch round his house as a defence, in case of being attacked. This would, however, have been of little avail if the Indians had come; but his chief comfort seemed to rest in the thought of selling his life dearly. A short time before, a body of Indians had travelled past in the night; if they had known of the posta, our black friend and his four soldiers would assuredly have been slaughtered. I did not anywhere meet a more civil and obliging man than this negro; it was therefore the more painful to see that he would not sit down and eat with us.

While in Brazil, not far from Itacaia, we passed under one of the massive, bare, and steep hills of granite which are so common in this country. This spot is notorious from having been, for a long time, the residence of some runaway slaves, who, by cultivating a little ground near the top, contrived to eke out a living. At length they were discovered,

A POST ON THE PAMPAS.

and a party of soldiers being sent, the whole were seized, with the exception of one old woman, who, sooner than again be led into slavery, dashed herself to pieces from the summit of the mountain. In a Roman matron this would have been called the noble love of freedom; in a poor negress it is mere brutal obstinacy.

During our stay at an estate on the river Macahe, I was very near being an eye-witness to one of those atrocious acts which can only take place in a slave country. Owing to a quarrel and a lawsuit, the owner was on the point of taking all the women and children from the male slaves, and selling them separately at the public auction at Rio. Self-interest, and not any feeling of pity, prevented this act. Indeed, I do not believe the inhumanity of separating thirty families, who had lived together for many years, ever occurred to the owner. Yet I will pledge myself that in humanity and good feeling he was better than the common run of men. It may be said there is no limit to the blindness of interest and selfish habit. I may mention one very trifling incident which, at the time, struck me more forcibly than any story of cruelty. I was crossing a ferry with a negro who was uncommonly stupid. In endeavoring to make him understand, I talked loud and made signs, in doing which I passed my hand near his face. He, I suppose, thought I was in a passion and was going to strike him, for instantly, with a frightened look and half-shut eyes, he dropped his hands. I shall never forget my feelings of surprise, disgust, and shame at seeing a great powerful man afraid even to ward off a blow, directed, as he thought, at his face. This man had been trained to a degradation lower than the slavery of the most helpless animal.

On the 19th of August, 1836, we finally left the shores of Brazil. I thank God I shall never again visit a slave country. To this day, if I hear a distant scream, it recalls with painful vividness my feelings when, passing a house near Pernambuco, I heard the most pitiable moans, and could not but suspect that some poor slave was being tortured, yet knew that I was as powerless as a child even to remonstrate. I suspected that these moans were from a tortured slave, for I was told that this was the case in another instance. Near Rio de Janeiro I lived opposite to an old lady who kept screws to crush the fingers of her female slaves. I have

PERNAMBUCO.

stayed in a house where a young household mulatto, daily and hourly, was reviled, beaten, and persecuted enough to break the spirit of the lowest animal. I have seen a little boy, six or seven years old, struck thrice with a horsewhip (before I could interfere) on his naked head, for having handed me a glass of water not quite clean. I saw his father tremble at a mere glance from his master's eye. These latter cruelties were witnessed by me in a Spanish colony, in which it has always been said that slaves are better treated than by the Portuguese, English, or other European nations. I will not even allude to the many heart-sickening atrocities which I heard of on good authority; nor would I have mentioned the above revolting details, had I not met with several people so blinded by the natural gayety of the negro as to speak of slavery as a tolerable evil. Such people have generally visited at the houses of the upper classes, where the domestic slaves are usually well treated—and they have not, like myself, lived among the lower classes. Such inquirers will ask slaves about their condition: they forget that the slave must indeed be dull who does not calculate on the chance of his answer reaching his master's ears.

It is argued that self-interest will prevent excessive cruelty; as if self-interest protected our domestic animals, which are far less likely than degraded slaves to stir up the rage of their savage masters. One day, riding in the Pampas with a very respectable planter (*estanciero*), my horse, being tired, lagged behind. The man often shouted to me to spur him. When I remonstrated that it was a pity, for the horse was quite exhausted, he cried out, "Why not? Never mind; spur him—it is *my* horse." I had then some difficulty in making him understand that it was for the horse's sake, and not on his account, that I did not choose to use my spurs. He exclaimed, with a look of great surprise, "Ah, Don Carlos, que cosa!" (what an idea). It was clear that such an idea had never before entered his head.

Those who look tenderly at the slave-owner, and with a cold heart at the slave, never seem to put themselves in the position of the latter. What a cheerless picture, with not even a hope of change! Picture to yourself the chance, ever hanging over you, of your wife and little children being torn from you and sold to the highest bidder! And these deeds are done and excused by men who profess to love their neighbors as themselves—who believe in God, and pray that his will be done on earth! It makes one's blood boil, yet heart tremble, to think that we Englishmen, and our American descendants, with their boastful cry of liberty, have been and are so guilty: but it is a consolation to reflect that we, at least, have made a greater sacrifice than was ever made by any nation to expiate our sin.*

THE GAUCHO.

At Las Minas we stopped overnight at a *pulperia*, or drinking-shop. During the evening a great number of Gauchos came in to drink spirits and smoke cigars. Their appearance is very striking: they are generally tall and handsome, but with a proud and dissolute expression of countenance. They often wear their mustaches, and long black hair curling down their backs. With their bright-colored garments, great spurs clanking about their heels, and knives stuck as daggers (and often so used) at their waists, they

* Slavery was finally abolished in the British West Indies in 1834–1838: in the United States by the civil war of 1861–1865.

look a different race of men from what might be expected from their name of *Gauchos*, or simple countrymen. Their politeness is excessive; they never drink their spirits without expecting you to taste it; but, while making their exceedingly graceful bow, they seem quite as ready, if occasion offered, to cut your throat.

THE GAUCHO.

The Gauchos are well known to be perfect riders. The idea of being thrown, let the horse do what it likes, never enters their head. Their test of a good rider is a man who can manage an untamed colt, or who, if his horse falls, alights on his own feet, or can perform other such exploits. I have heard of a man betting that he would throw his horse down twenty times, and that nineteen times he would not fall himself. I recollect seeing a Gaucho riding a very stubborn horse, which three times in succession reared so high as to fall backward with great violence. The man judged with uncommon coolness the proper moment for slipping off—not an instant before or after the right time—and as soon as the horse got up the man jumped on his back, and at last they started at a gallop. The Gaucho never appears to exert any muscular force. I was one day watching a good rider, as we were galloping along at a rapid pace, and thought to myself, "Surely, if the horse starts, you appear so careless on your seat, you must fall." At this moment a male ostrich sprung from its nest right beneath the horse's nose. The young colt bounded on one side like a stag; but as for the man, all that could be said was that he started and took fright with his horse. I was surprised to hear the Gauchos, who have from infancy almost lived on horseback, say that they always suffered from stiffness when, not having ridden for some time, they first began again. One of them told me that, having been confined for three months by illness, he went out hunting wild cattle, and, in consequence, for the next ten days his thighs were so stiff that he was obliged to lie in bed. This shows that the Gauchos must really exert much muscular effort in riding.

In Chile and Peru more pains are taken with the mouth of the horse than in La Plata, evidently because of the more intricate nature of the country. In Chile a horse is not considered perfectly broken till he can be brought up standing, in the midst of his full speed, on any particular spot—for instance, on a cloak thrown on the ground: or, again, he will charge a wall, and rearing, scrape the surface with his hoofs. I have seen an animal bounding with spirit, yet merely reined by a forefinger and thumb, taken at full gallop across a court-yard, then made to wheel round the post of a veranda with great speed, but at so equal a distance that the rider, with outstretched arm, all the while kept one finger rubbing the post; then making a demivolt in the air, with the man's other arm outstretched in a like manner, he wheeled round, with astonishing force, in an opposite direction.

NOT TO BE THROWN.

Such a horse is well broken: and although this at first may appear useless, it is far otherwise. It is only carrying to perfection a daily necessity. When a bullock is checked and caught by the *lazo*, it will sometimes gallop round and round in a circle; and the horse, being alarmed at the great strain, if not well broken, will not readily turn like the pivot of a wheel. In consequence, many men have been killed; for if the lazo once takes a twist round a man's body, it will instantly, from the power of the two opposed animals, almost cut him in twain. A man on horseback, having thrown his lazo round the horns of a beast, can drag it anywhere he chooses. The animal, ploughing up the ground with outstretched legs, in vain efforts to resist the force, generally dashes at full speed to one side; but the horse, immediately turning to receive the shock, stands so firmly that the bullock is almost thrown down, and it is surprising that their necks are not broken. The struggle is not, however, one of fair strength, since the horse's girth is matched against the bullock's extended neck. In a similar manner a man can hold the wildest horse, if caught with the lazo just behind the ears.

The lazo is a very strong, but thin, well-plaited rope, made of raw hide. One end is attached to the broad surcingle which fastens together the complicated gear of the *recado*, or saddle used in the Pampas; at the other end is a small ring of iron or brass, by which a noose can be formed. The Gaucho, when he is going to use the lazo, keeps a small coil in his bridle-hand, and in the other holds the running noose, which is made very large, generally having a diameter of about eight feet. This he whirls round his head, and by the dexterous movement of his wrist keeps the noose open; then, throwing it, he causes it to fall on any particular spot he chooses. The lazo, when not used, is tied up in a small coil to the after part of the recado.

The bolas, or balls, are of two kinds. The simplest, which are chiefly used for catching ostriches, consist of two round stones, covered with leather, and united by a thin plaited thong about eight feet long. The other kind differs only in having three balls united by the thong to a common centre. The Gaucho holds the smallest of the three in his hand, and whirls the other two round and round his head; then, taking aim, sends them like chain-shot whirling through the air. The balls no sooner strike any object than, winding round it, they cross each other, and become firmly hitched. The size and weight of the balls vary, according to the purpose for which they are made: when of stone, although not larger than an English apple, they are sent with such force as sometimes to break the legs even of a horse. I have seen the balls made of wood, and as large as a turnip, for the sake of catching these animals without injuring them. The balls are sometimes made of iron, and these can be hurled to the greatest distance.

The main difficulty in using either lazo or bolas is to ride so well as to be able at full speed, and while suddenly turning about, to whirl them so steadily round the head as to take aim: on foot, any person would soon learn the art. One day, as I was amusing myself by galloping and whirling the balls round my head, by accident the free one struck a bush, and its revolving motion being thus destroyed, it immediately fell to the ground, and like magic caught one hind leg of my horse; the other ball was then jerked out of my hand, and the horse fairly secured. Luckily he was an old practised animal, and knew what it meant, otherwise he

USE OF LAZO AND BOLAS.

would probably have kicked till he had thrown himself down. The Gauchos roared with laughter; they cried out that they had seen every sort of animal caught, but had never before seen a man caught by himself.

About two leagues beyond the curious tree of Walleechu we halted for the night. At this instant an unfortunate cow was spied by the lynx-eyed Gauchos, who set off in full chase, and in a few minutes dragged her in with their lazos and slaughtered her. We here had the four necessaries of life in the open plain (*en el campo*)—pasture for the horses, water (only a muddy puddle), meat, and firewood. The Gauchos were in high spirits at finding all these luxuries, and we soon set to work at the poor cow. This was the first night which I passed under the open sky, with the saddle-gear for my bed. There is high enjoyment in the independence of the Gaucho life—to be able at any moment to pull up your horse and say, "Here we will pass the night." The death-like stillness of the plain, the dogs keeping watch, the gypsy group of Gauchos making their beds round the fire, have left in my mind a strongly-marked picture of this first night, which will never be forgotten.

At Tapulquen we were able to buy some biscuit. I had now been several days without tasting anything beside meat. I did not at all dislike this new diet, but I felt as if it would only have agreed with me with hard exercise. I have heard that patients in England, to whom an exclusively animal diet has been prescribed, have hardly been able to endure it, even to save their lives; yet the Gauchos in the Pampas, for months together, touch nothing but beef. But they eat, I observe, a very large proportion of fat, and they particularly dislike dry meat, such as that of the agouti. It is, perhaps, on account of their meat diet that the Gauchos, like other flesh-eating animals, can long go without food. I was told of some troops who, of their own accord, pursued a party of Indians for three days, without eating or drinking.

One night in the Falkland Islands we slept on the neck of land at the head of Choiseul Sound, which forms the south-west peninsula. The valley was pretty well sheltered from the cold wind; but there was very little brushwood for fuel. The Gauchos, however, soon found what, to my great surprise, made nearly as hot a fire as coals; this was the skeleton of a bullock lately killed, from which the flesh had been picked by the carrion-hawks. They told me that in winter they often killed a beast, cleaned the flesh from the bones with their knives, and then with these same bones roasted the meat for their supper.

THE AGOUTI.

THE LA PLATAN.

At Santa Fé I was confined for two days to my bed by a headache. A good-natured old woman, who attended me, wished me to try many odd remedies. A common practice is to bind an orange-leaf or a bit of black plaster to each temple; and a still more general plan is to split a bean into halves, moisten them, and place one on each temple, where they will easily stick. It is not thought proper ever to remove the bean or plaster, but to let them drop off; and sometimes, if a man with patches on his head is asked what is the matter, he will answer, "I had a headache the day before yesterday."

THE URUGUAYAN.

On the first night out from Maldonado we slept at a retired little country-house, and there I soon found out that I owned two or three articles, especially a pocket compass, which created unbounded astonishment. In every house I was asked to show the compass, and by its aid, together with a map, to point out the direction of various places. It excited the liveliest admiration that I, a perfect stranger, should know the road (for direction and road mean the same thing in this open country) to places where I had never been. At one house a young woman, who was ill in bed, sent to beg me to come and show her the compass. If their surprise was great, mine was greater to find such ignorance among people owning thousands of cattle, and *estancias* of great extent. It can only be explained by the circumstance that this retired part of the country is seldom visited by foreigners. I was asked whether the earth or sun moved; whether it was hotter or colder to the north; where Spain was, and many other such questions. The greater number of the inhabitants had an indistinct idea that England, London, and North America were different names for the same place; but the better informed well knew that London and North America were separate countries, close together, and that England was a large town in London! I carried with me some promethean matches, which I lighted by biting; it was thought so wonderful that a man should strike fire with his teeth that it was usual to collect the whole family to see it. I was once offered a dollar for a single one! Washing my face in the morning caused much speculation at the village of Las Minas. A superior tradesman closely cross-questioned me about so singular a practice, and likewise why, on board ship, we wore our beards (for he had heard from my guide that we did so). He eyed me with much suspicion. It is the general custom in this country to ask for a night's lodging at the first convenient house. The astonishment at the compass and my other feats in jugglery was a certain advantage to me, as with that, and the long stories my guides told of my breaking stones, knowing venomous from harmless snakes, collecting insects, etc., I repaid them for their hospitality. I am writing as if I had been among the inhabitants of Central Africa. Banda Oriental would not be flattered by the comparison, but such were my feelings at the time.

On the road toward Mercedes, on the Rio Negro, we asked leave to sleep at an estancia at which we happened to arrive. It was a very large estate, being ten leagues square; and the owner is one of the greatest land-owners in the country. His nephew had charge of it, and with him there was a captain in the army, who the other day ran away from Buenos Ayres. Considering their station, their conversation was rather amusing. They expressed, as was usual, unbounded astonishment at the globe being round, and could scarcely believe that a hole would, if deep enough, come out on the other side. They had, however, heard of a country where there were six months of light and six of darkness, and where the inhabitants were very tall and thin! They were curious about the price and condition of horses and cattle in England. Upon finding that we did not catch our animals with the lazo, they cried out: "Ah, then, you use nothing but the bolas!" The idea of an enclosed country was quite new to them. The captain at last said he had one question to ask me, which he should be very much obliged if I would answer with all truth: it was, "Whether the ladies of Buenos Ayres were not the handsomest in the world." I replied, "Charm-

AN ESTANCIERO (PLANTER).

ingly so." He added, "I have one other question: Do ladies in any other part of the world wear such large combs?" I solemnly assured him that they did not. They were absolutely delighted. The captain exclaimed, "Look there! a man who has seen half the world says it is the case; we always thought so, but now we know it." My excellent judgment in combs and beauty procured me a most hospitable reception. The captain forced me to take his bed, and would sleep on his recado.

At Mercedes I asked two men why they did not work. One gravely said the days were too long; the other, that he was too poor. The number of horses and the abundance of food are the destruction of all industry. Moreover, there are so many feast-days: and again, nothing can succeed unless it be begun when the moon is on the increase; so that half the month is lost from these two causes.

Both at Colonia and in other places I noticed a very general interest in the approaching election for President. The inhabitants do not require much education in their representatives. I heard some men discussing the merits of those for Colonia, and it was said that, "although they were not men of business, they could all sign their names." With this they seemed to think every reasonable man ought to be satisfied.

THE CHILENO.

I MUST express my admiration at the natural politeness of almost every Chileno. I may mention an incident with which I was at the time much pleased: We met near Mendoza a little and very fat negress riding astride on a mule. She had a goitre so enormous that it was scarcely possible to avoid gazing at her for a moment; but my two companions (Chilians) almost instantly, by way of apology, made the common salute of the country by taking off their hats. Where would one of the lower or higher classes in Europe have shown such feeling politeness to a poor and miserable object of a degraded race?

My geological examination of the country generally caused a good deal of surprise among the Chilenos: it was long before they could be convinced that I was not hunting for mines. This was sometimes troublesome. I found the readiest way of explaining my employment was to ask them how it was that they themselves were not curious concerning earthquakes and volcanoes?—why some springs were hot and others cold?—why there were mountains in Chile and not a hill in La Plata? These bare questions at once satisfied and silenced the greater number; some, however (like a few in England who are a century behind), thought that all such inquiries were useless and impious, and that it was quite sufficient that God had thus made the mountains.

The Chilian miners are a peculiar race of men in their habits. Living for weeks together in the most desolate spots, when they descend to the villages on feast-days there is no excess or extravagance into which they do not run. They sometimes gain a considerable sum, and then, like sailors with prize-money, they try how soon they can contrive to squander it. They drink excessively, buy quantities of clothes, and in a few days return penniless to their miserable abodes, there to work harder than beasts of burden. This thoughtlessness, as with sailors, is evidently the result of a similar mode of life. Their daily food is found for them, and they acquire no habits of carefulness; moreover, temptation and the means of yielding to it are placed in their power at the same time. On the other hand, in Cornwall, and some other parts of

England, where the system of selling part of the vein is followed, the miners are obliged to act and think for themselves, and are therefore a singularly intelligent and well-behaved set of men.

The dress of the Chilian miner is peculiar and rather picturesque. He wears a very long shirt of some dark-colored baize, with a leathern apron, the whole being fastened round his waist by a bright-colored sash. His trousers are very broad, and his small cap of scarlet cloth is made to fit the head closely. We met a party of these miners in full costume, carrying the body of one of their companions to be buried. They marched at a very quick trot, four men supporting the corpse. One set having run as hard as they could for about two hundred yards, were relieved by four others, who had previously dashed ahead on horseback. Thus they proceeded, encouraging each other by wild cries. Altogether the scene formed a most strange funeral.

Captain Head has described the wonderful load which the "apires"—truly beasts of burden—carry up from the deepest mines. I confess I thought the account exaggerated, so that I was glad to take an opportunity of weighing one of the loads, which I picked out by hazard. It required considerable exertion on my part, when standing directly over it, to lift it from the ground. The load was considered under weight when found to be one hundred and ninety-seven pounds. The apire had carried this up eighty perpendicular yards—part of the way by a steep passage, but the greater part up notched poles, placed in a zigzag line up the shaft. According to rule, the apire is not allowed to halt for breath unless the mine is six hundred feet deep. The average load is considered as rather more than two hundred pounds, and I have been assured that one of three hundred pounds, by way of a trial, had been brought up from the deepest mine. At this time the apires were bringing up the usual load twelve times in the day—that is, twenty-four hundred pounds from eighty yards deep; and they were employed in the intervals in breaking and picking ore.

TANATERO—ORE CARRIER.

These men, excepting from accidents, are healthy, and appear cheerful. Their bodies are not very muscular. They rarely eat meat once a week, and never oftener. Although knowing that their labor was not forced, it was nevertheless quite revolting to see the state in which they reached the mouth of the mine—their bodies bent forward, their legs bowed, their muscles quivering, the perspiration streaming from their faces over their breasts, their nostrils distended, the corners of their mouths forcibly drawn back, and the expulsion of their breath most laborious. After staggering to the pile of ore, they emptied the *carpacho;* in two or three seconds recovering their breath, they wiped the sweat from their brows, and, apparently quite fresh, descended the mine again at a quick pace. This seems to me a wonderful instance of the amount of labor which habit, for it can be nothing else, will enable a man to endure.

THE SPANIARD.

One day, while we were at the gold-mines of Yaquil, a German collector in natural history, of the name of Renous, called, and nearly at the same time an old Spanish lawyer. I was amused at being told the conversation which took place between them. Renous speaks Spanish so well that the old lawyer mistook him for a Chilian. Renous, alluding to me, asked him what he thought of the King of England sending out a collector to their country, to pick up lizards and beetles, and to break stones. The old gentleman thought seriously for some time, and then said, "It is not well—*hay un gato encerrado aquí* (there is a cat shut up here). No man is so rich as to send out people to pick up such rubbish. I do not like it. If one of us were to go and do such things in England, do not you think the King of England would very soon send us out of his country?" And this old gentleman, from his profession, belongs to the better informed and more intelligent classes! Renous himself, two or three years before, left in a house at San Fernando some caterpillars, under charge of a girl to feed, that they might turn into butterflies. This was rumored through the town, and at last the priests and the governor consulted together, and agreed it must be some heresy. So, when Renous returned, he was arrested.

TAMARIND-TREE AT POINT VENUS, TAHITI, SOCIETY ISLANDS

The captain with whom we descended the river Parana was an old Spaniard, and had been many years in South America. He professed a great liking for the English, but stoutly maintained that the battle of Trafalgar was merely won by the Spanish captains having been all bought over, and that the only really gallant action on either side was performed by the Spanish admiral. It struck me as rather characteristic that this man should prefer his countrymen being thought the worst of traitors, rather than unskilful or cowardly.

THE TAHITIAN.

At Tahiti I was pleased with nothing so much as with the inhabitants. There is a mildness in the expression of their countenances which at once banishes the idea of a savage, and an intelligence which shows that they are advancing in civilization. The common people, when working, keep the upper part of their bodies quite naked; and it is then that the Tahitians are seen to advantage. They are very tall, broad-shouldered, athletic, and well-proportioned. It has been remarked that it requires little habit to make a dark skin more pleasing and natural to the eye of a European than his own color. A white man, bathing by the side of a Tahitian, was like a plant bleached by the gardener's art compared with a fine dark green one, growing vigorously in the open fields. Most of the men are tattooed, and the ornaments follow the curves of the body so gracefully that they have a very elegant effect. One common pattern, varying in its details, is somewhat like the crown of a palm-tree. It springs from the central line of the back, and gracefully curls round both sides. Many of the elder people had their feet covered with small figures, so placed as to resemble a sock. This fashion, however, is partly gone by. The women are tattooed in the same manner as the men, and very commonly

NATIVE BAMBOO HOUSE, TAHITI, SOCIETY ISLANDS.

on their fingers. They are far inferior, in every respect, to the men.

On a short excursion into the mountains our line of march was the valley of Tia-auru, down which a river flows into the sea by Point Venus. We bivouacked for the night on a flat little spot on the bank of one of the streams into which the river divided itself at its head. The Tahitians, in a few minutes, built us an excellent house, and then proceeded to make a fire and cook our evening meal. A light was procured by rubbing a blunt-pointed stick in a groove made in another, as if in order to deepen it, until by the friction the dust was ignited. A peculiarly white and very light wood is alone used for this purpose. The fire was produced in a few seconds; but, to a person who does not understand the art, it requires, as I found, the greatest exertion; but at last, to my great pride, I succeeded in igniting the dust. The Gaucho in the Pampas uses a different method: taking an elastic stick, about eighteen inches long, he presses one end on his breast, and the other pointed end into a hole in a piece of wood, and then rapidly turns the curved part, like a carpenter's centre-bit. The Tahitians, having made a small fire of sticks, placed a score of stones,

FIRE BY FRICTION.

BANANA LEAVES AND FRUIT-STALK.

of about the size of cricket-balls, on the burning wood. In about ten minutes the sticks were consumed, and the stones hot. They had previously folded up in small parcels of leaves pieces of beef, fish, ripe and unripe bananas, and the tops of the wild arum. These green parcels were laid in a layer between two layers of the hot stones, and the whole then covered up with earth, so that no smoke or steam could escape. In about a quarter of an hour the whole was most deliciously cooked. The choice green parcels were now laid on a cloth of banana leaves, and with a cocoa-nut shell we drank the cool water of the running stream; and thus we enjoyed our rustic meal.

BANANA BLOSSOM.

THE AUSTRALIAN NEGRO.

A LARGE tribe of natives, called the White Cockatoo men, happened to pay a visit to the settlement at King George's Sound while we were there. These men, as well as those of the tribe belonging to the Sound, being tempted by the offer of some tubs of rice and sugar, were persuaded to hold a "corrobery," or great dancing-party. As soon as it grew dark, small fires were lighted and the men commenced their toilet, which consisted in painting themselves white in spots and lines. As soon as all was ready, large fires were kept blazing, round which the women and children were collected as spectators. The Cockatoo and King George's men formed two distinct parties, and generally danced in answer to each other. The dancing consisted in their running, either sideways or in Indian file, into an open space, and stamping the ground with great force as they marched together. Their heavy footsteps were accompanied by a kind of grunt, by beating their clubs and spears together, and by various other gesticulations, such as extending their arms and wriggling their bodies. It was a most rude, barbarous scene, and, to our ideas, without any sort of meaning; but we observed that the black women and children watched it with the greatest pleasure. Perhaps these dances originally represented actions, such as wars and victories. There was one called the Emu dance, in which each man extended his arm in a

AUSTRALIAN NEGRO.

THE KANGAROO.

bent manner, like the neck of that bird. In another dance, one man imitated the movements of a kangaroo grazing in the woods, while a second crawled up and pretended to spear him. When both tribes mingled in the dance the ground trembled with the heaviness of their steps, and the air resounded with their wild cries. Every one appeared in high spirits; and the group of nearly naked figures, viewed by the light of the blazing fires, all moving in hideous harmony, formed a perfect display of a festival among the lowest barbarians. In Tierra del Fuego we had beheld many curious scenes in savage life, but never, I think, one where the natives were in such high spirits and so perfectly at their ease. After the dancing was over, the whole party formed a great circle on the ground, and the boiled rice and sugar was distributed, to the delight of all.

AUSTRALIAN "CORROBERY."

III.

GEOGRAPHY.

M. BONPLAND.

URUGUAY.

SOUTH AMERICA.

THE general and almost entire absence of trees in Banda Oriental (or Uruguay) is remarkable. Some of the rocky hills are partly covered by thickets, and on the banks of the larger streams, especially to the north of Las Minas, willow-trees are not uncommon. Near the Arroyo Tapes I heard of a wood of palms; and one of these trees, of considerable size, I saw near the Pan de Azucar (Sugar-Loaf), in latitude thirty-five degrees. These, and the trees planted by the Spaniards, offer the only exceptions to the general scarcity of wood. Among the introduced kinds may be enumerated poplars, olives, peach, and other fruit-trees: the peaches succeed so well that they

OLIVE BRANCH.

MONTEVIDEO.

afford the main supply of firewood to the city of Buenos Ayres. Extremely level countries, such as the Pampas, seldom appear favorable to the growth of trees.

RIVER PARANA.

The Parana is full of islands, which undergo a constant round of decay and renovation. In the memory of the master of our *balandra* (one-masted vessel) several large ones had disappeared, and others again had been formed and protected by vegetation. They are composed of muddy sand, without even the smallest pebble, and were then about four feet above the level of the river; but during the periodical floods they are overflowed. They all have one character: numerous willow and a few other trees are bound together by a great variety of creeping plants, thus forming a thick jungle. These thickets afford a retreat for capybaras and jaguars. The fear of the latter animal quite destroyed all pleasure in scrambling through the woods. On every island there were tracks. In the evening the mosquitoes were very troublesome. I exposed my hand for five minutes, and it was soon black with them; I do not suppose that there could have been less than fifty, all busy sucking.

Some leagues below Rosario the western shore of the Parana is bounded by perpendicular cliffs, which extend in a long line to below San Nicolas; hence it more resembles a sea-coast than that of a fresh-water river. It is a great drawback to the scenery of the Parana that, from the soft nature of its banks, the water is very muddy. The Uruguay, flowing through a granitic country, is much clearer; and, where the two channels unite at the head of the Plata, the waters may for a long distance be distinguished by their black and red colors. We met during our descent very few vessels. One of the best gifts of nature, in so grand a channel of communication, seems here wilfully thrown away—a river in which ships might navigate from a temperate country as surprisingly abundant in certain productions as destitute of others, to another possessing a tropical climate and a soil which, according to the best of judges, M. Bonpland, is perhaps unequalled in fertility in any part of the world. How different would have been the aspect of this river if English colonists had by good-fortune first sailed up the Plata! What noble towns would now have occupied its shores!

THE PLATE RIVER.

Having been delayed for nearly a fortnight in Buenos Ayres, I was glad to escape on board a packet bound for

THE CITY OF MONTEVIDEO, LOOKING TOWARD THE HARBOR.

Montevideo. Our passage was a very long and tedious one. The Plata looks like a noble estuary on the map, but is in truth a poor affair. A wide expanse of muddy water has neither grandeur nor beauty. At one time of the day the two shores, both of which are extremely low, could just be distinguished from the deck.

LA PLATA.

In the evening of September 27, 1833, I set out from Buenos Ayres for Sante Fé, situated nearly three hundred

English miles distant, on the banks of the Parana. The roads in the neighborhood of the city, after the rainy weather, were extraordinarily bad. I should never have thought it possible for a bullock wagon to have crawled along; as it was, they scarcely went at the rate of a mile an hour, and a man was kept ahead to select the best line for making the attempt. The bullocks were terribly jaded: it is a great mistake to suppose that, with improved roads and a quickened rate of travelling, the sufferings of the animals increase in the same proportion. We passed a train of wagons and a troop of beasts on their road to Mendoza. The distance is about five hundred and eighty geographical miles, and the journey is generally performed in fifty days. These wagons are very long and narrow, and thatched with reeds; they have only two wheels, the diameter of which is in some cases as much as ten feet. Each is drawn by six bullocks, which are urged on by a goad at least twenty feet long; this is hung from within the roof: for the wheel bullocks a smaller one is kept; and for the middle pair a point projects at right angles from the middle of the long one. The whole apparatus looked like some implement of war.

At San Nicolas I first saw the noble river of the Parana. At the foot of the cliff on which the town stands some large vessels were at anchor. Before arriving at Rosario we crossed the Saladillo, a stream of fine, clear, running water, but too salty to drink. Rosario is a large town built on a dead level plain, which forms a cliff about sixty feet high over the Parana. The river here is very broad, with many islands, which are low and wooded, as is also the opposite shore. The view would resemble that of a great lake if it were not for the linear-shaped islets, which alone give the idea of running water. The cliffs are the most picturesque part; sometimes they are absolutely perpendicular, and of a red color; at other times in large broken masses, covered with cacti and mimosa trees.

For many leagues north and south of San Nicolas and

OX-CART OF THE PAMPAS.

Rosario the country is really level. Scarcely anything which travellers have written about its extreme flatness can be con sidered as exaggeration. Yet I could never find a spot where, by slowly turning round, objects were not seen at greater distances in some directions than in others; and this manifestly proves inequality in the plain. At sea, if a person's eye is six feet above the surface of the water, his horizon is two miles and four-fifths distant. In like manner, the more level the plain, the more nearly does the horizon approach within these narrow limits; and this, in my opinion, entirely destroys that grandeur which one would have imagined that a vast level plain would have possessed.

THE PAMPAS.

The view from the post of Cufre, in Banda Oriental, was pleasing: an undulating green surface, with distant glimpses of the Plata. I find that I look at this province with very different eyes from what I did upon my first arrival. I recollect I then thought it singularly level; but now (November, 1833), after galloping over the Pampas, my only surprise is, what could have induced me ever to have called it level. The country is a series of undulations, in themselves, perhaps, not absolutely great, but, as compared to the plains of Santa Fé, real mountains. From these unevennesses there is an abundance of small rivulets, and the turf is green and luxuriant.

The number of the animal remains imbedded in the grand estuary deposit which forms the Pampas, and covers the granitic rocks of Banda Oriental, must be extraordinarily great. I believe a straight line drawn in any direction through the Pampas would cut through some skeleton or bones. Besides those which I found, during my short excursions, I heard of many others, and the origin of such names as "The stream of the animal," "The hill of the giant," is obvious. At other times I heard of the marvellous property of certain rivers, which had the power of changing small bones into large; or, as some maintained, the bones themselves grew. As far as I am aware, not one of these animals perished, as was formerly supposed, in the marshes or river beds of the present land, but their bones have been exposed by streams cutting through the watery deposit in which they were originally imbedded. We may conclude that the whole area of the Pampas is one wide sepulchre of extinct gigantic quadrupeds.

In calling up images of the past, I find that the plains of Patagonia frequently cross before my eyes; yet these plains are pronounced by everybody wretched and useless. Without habitations, without water, without trees, without mountains, they support merely a few dwarf plants. Why then have these arid wastes taken so firm a hold on my memory, and not on mine alone? Why have not the still more level, the greener and more fertile Pampas, which are more serviceable to mankind, produced an equal impression? I can scarcely analyze these feelings, but it must be partly owing to the free scope given to the imagination. The plains of Patagonia are boundless, for they are scarcely passable, and hence unknown; they bear the stamp of having lasted, as they are now, for ages, and there appears no limit to their duration through future time. If, as the ancients supposed, the flat earth was surrounded by an impassable breadth of water, or by deserts heated to an unbearable excess, who would not look at these lost boundaries to man's knowledge with deep but vague sensations?

TIERRA DEL FUEGO.

Tierra del Fuego may be described as a mountainous land, partly sunk in the sea, so that deep inlets and bays occupy the place where valleys should exist. The mountain sides, except on the exposed western coast, are covered from the water's edge upward by one great forest. The trees reach to an elevation of between one thousand and fifteen hundred feet, and are succeeded by a band of peat with tiny alpine plants; and this again is succeeded by the line of perpetual snow. To find an acre of level land in any part of the country is most rare. I recollect only one little flat piece near Port Famine, and another of rather larger extent near Goeree Road. In both places, and everywhere else, the surface is covered by a thick bed of swampy peat. Even within the forest the ground is hidden by a mass of slowly rotting vegetable matter, which, from being soaked with water, yields to the foot. The trees all belong to one kind, the *Fagus betuloides*. This beech keeps its leaves throughout the year, but its foliage is of a peculiar brownish green color, with a tinge of yellow. As the whole landscape is thus colored, it has a sombre, dull appearance; nor is it often enlivened by the rays of the sun.

On the morning of the 28th of January, 1833, Captain Fitz Roy determined to proceed with two boats to survey the western parts of Beagle Channel. The day, to our astonishment, was overpoweringly hot, so that our skins were scorched. With this beautiful weather the view in the middle of the channel was very remarkable. Looking toward either hand, no object interrupted the perspective of this long canal between the mountains. We sailed on till it was dark, and then pitched our tents in a quiet creek on a beach of pebbles, where, in our blanket-bags, we passed a most comfortable night. Early in the morning of the next day we

MOUNTAINS AND GLACIERS IN MAGELLAN STRAITS.

reached the point where the Beagle Channel divides into two arms, and we entered the northern one. The scenery here becomes even grander than before. The lofty mountains on the north side, forming the granite axis or backbone of the country, boldly rise to a height of between three and four thousand feet, with one peak above six thousand feet. They are covered by a wide mantle of perpetual snow, and numerous cascades pour their waters through the woods into the narrow channel below. In many parts magnificent glaciers extend from the mountain side to the water's edge. It is scarcely possible to imagine anything more beautiful than the beryl-like blue of these glaciers, especially in contrast with the dead white of the upper expanse of snow. The fragments which had fallen from the glacier into the water were floating away, and the channel with its icebergs presented, for the space of a mile, a miniature likeness of the Polar Sea.

The boats being hauled on shore at our dinner-hour, we were admiring from the distance of half a mile a perpendicular cliff of ice, and were wishing that some more fragments would fall. At last down came a mass with a roaring noise, and immediately we saw the smooth outline of a wave travelling toward us. The men ran down as quickly as they could to the boats, for the chance of their being dashed to pieces was evident. One of the seamen just caught hold of the bows as the curling breaker reached it: he was knocked over and over, but not hurt, and the boats, though thrice lifted on high and let fall again, received no damage. This was most fortunate for us, for we were a hundred miles distant from the ship, and we should have been left without provisions or fire-arms.

CHILOE.

EARLY on Sunday morning, November 30, 1834, we reached Castro, the ancient capital of Chiloe, but now a most forlorn and deserted place. The usual quadrangular arrangement of Spanish towns could be traced, but the streets and *plaza* (public square) were coated with fine green turf, on which sheep were browsing. The church, which stands in the middle, is entirely built of plank, and has a picturesque and venerable appearance. The poverty of the place may be imagined from the fact that, although containing some hundreds of inhabitants, one of our party was unable anywhere to purchase either a pound of sugar or an ordinary knife. No person possessed either a watch or a clock; and an old man, who was supposed to have a good idea of time, was employed to strike the church bell by guess. The arrival of our boats was a rare event in this quiet, retired corner of the world; and nearly all the inhabitants came down to the beach to see us pitch our tents.

VALPARAISO.

THE *Beagle* anchored late at night (July 23, 1834) in the bay of Valparaiso, the chief seaport of Chile. When morn-

CUSTOMS GUARD-HOUSE, VALPARAISO, CHILE.

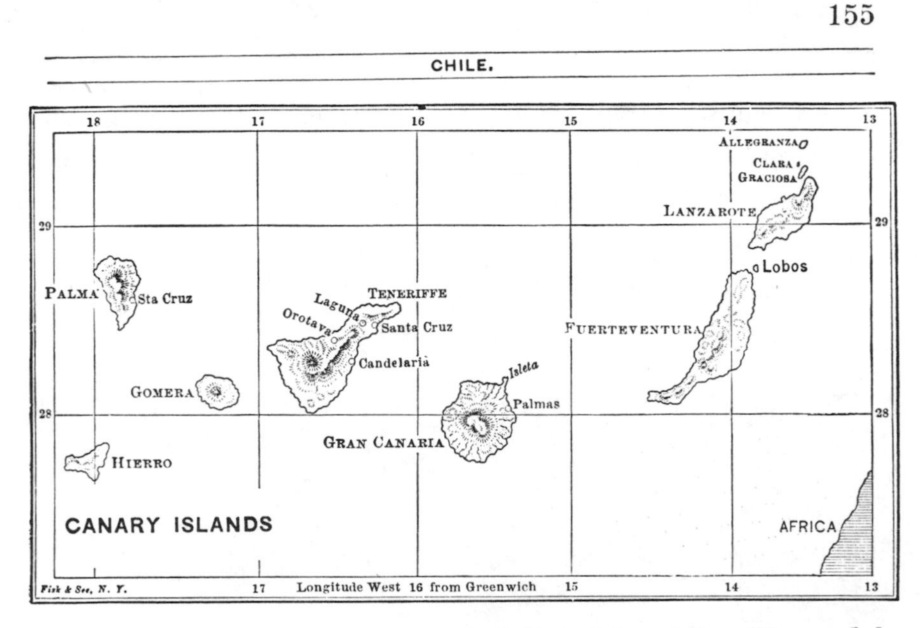

ing came, everything appeared delightful. After Tierra del Fuego the climate felt quite delicious—the atmosphere so dry, and the heavens so clear and blue, with the sun shining brightly, that all nature seemed sparkling with life. The view from the anchorage is very pretty. The town is built

PLAZA DE LA CONSTITUCION, SANTA CRUZ.

at the foot of a range of hills, about sixteen hundred feet high, and rather steep. From its position it consists of one long straggling street, which runs parallel to the beach, and wherever a ravine comes down the houses are piled up on each side of it. The rounded hills, being only partially protected by a very scanty vegetation, are worn into numberless little gullies, which expose a singularly bright red soil. From this cause, and from the low whitewashed houses with tile

PEAK OF TENERIFFE.

roofs, the view reminded me of Santa Cruz in Teneriffe. In a north-easterly direction there are some fine glimpses of the Andes, but these mountains appear much grander when viewed from the neighboring hills: the great distance at which they are situated can then more readily be perceived. The volcano of Aconcagua is particularly magnificent; its height is no less than twenty-three thousand feet.

QUILLOTA.

Whoever called Valparaiso the "Valley of Paradise" must have been thinking of Quillota. Any one who had seen only the country near Valparaiso would never have imagined that there had been such picturesque spots in Chile.

ORANGE-GROVES.

As soon as we reached the brow of the sierra the valley of Quillota was immediately under our feet: very broad and quite flat, and easily irrigated in all parts. The little square gardens are crowded with orange and olive trees, and every sort of vegetable. On each side huge bare mountains rise, and the contrast renders the patchwork valley the more pleasing.

VALDIVIA.

VALDIVIA is situated about ten miles from the coast, on the low banks of a stream, and is so completely buried in a wood of apple-trees that the streets are merely paths in an orchard. I have never seen any country where apple-trees appeared to thrive so well as in this damp part of South America: on the borders of the roads there were many young trees, evidently self-sown. In the island of Chiloe the inhabitants have a marvellously short method of making an orchard. At the lower part of almost every branch small conical brown wrinkled points project; these are always ready to change into roots, as may sometimes be seen where any mud has been accidentally splashed against the tree. A branch as thick as a man's thigh is chosen in the early spring, and is cut off just beneath a group of these points; all the smaller branches are lopped off, and it is then placed about two feet deep in the ground. During the next summer the stump throws out long shoots, and sometimes even bears fruit. I was shown one which had produced as many as twenty-three apples, but this was thought very unusual. In the third season the stump is changed (as I have myself seen) into a well-wooded tree, loaded with fruit. An old man near Valdivia gave us an account of the several useful things he manufactured from his apples. After making cider, and likewise wine, he extracted from the leavings a white and finely-flavored spirit; by another process he procured a sweet treacle, or, as he called it, honey. His children and pigs seemed almost to live, during this season of the year, in his orchard.

CHILE.

Chile, as may be seen in the maps, is a narrow strip of land between the Cordillera and the Pacific; and this strip is itself traversed by several mountain-lines, which, near Quillota, run parallel to the great range. Between these outer lines and the main Cordillera a succession of level basins, generally opening into each other by narrow passages, extend far to the southward: in these the principal towns are situated, as San Felipe, Santiago, San Fernando. These basins or plains, together with the flat cross-valleys (like that of Quillota) which connect them with the coast, I have no doubt are the bottoms of ancient inlets and deep bays, such as at the present day intersect every part of Tierra del Fuego and the western coast. The resemblance of Chile to the latter country was occasionally shown strikingly when a level fog-bank covered, as with a mantle, all the lower parts of the country; the white vapor curling into the ravines beautifully represented little coves and bays, and here and there a solitary hillock peeping up, showed that it had formerly stood there as an islet.

LIMA.

Lima stands on a plain in a valley formed during the gradual retreat of the sea. It is seven miles from Callao, and five hundred feet higher; but, from the slope being very gradual, the road appears absolutely level, so that when at Lima it is difficult to believe one has ascended even one

LIMA.

hundred feet. Steep barren hills rise like islands from the plain, which is divided by straight mud-walls into large green fields. In these scarcely a tree grows excepting a few willows, and an occasional clump of bananas and oranges. Lima,

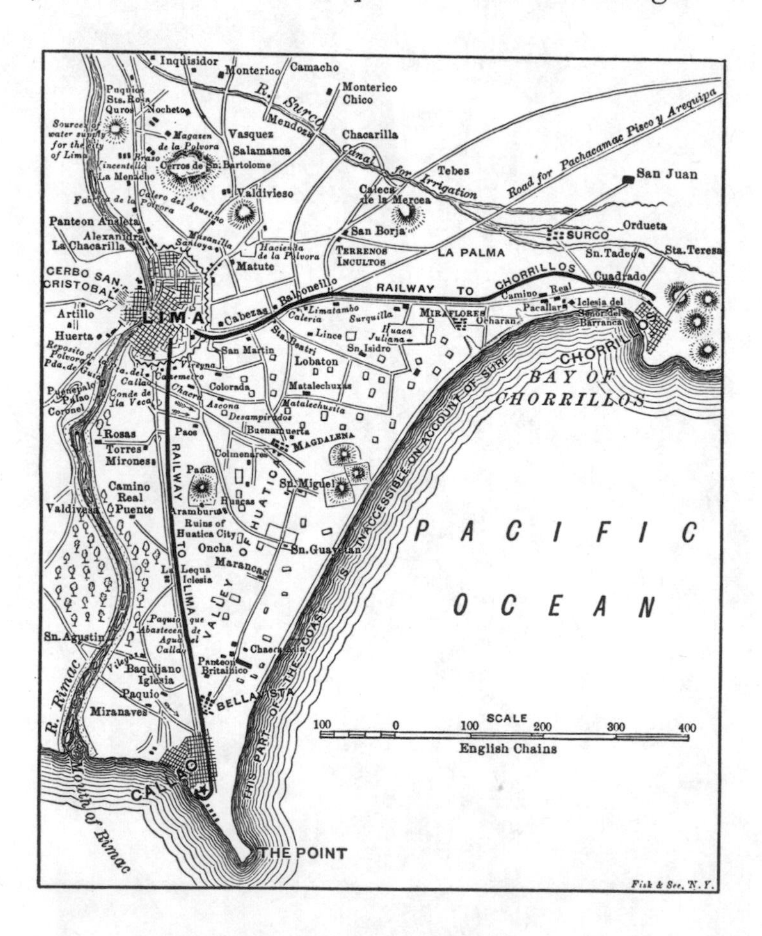

the "City of the Kings," must formerly have been a splendid town. The extraordinary number of churches gives it, even at the present day, a peculiar and striking character, especially when viewed from a short distance.

One day I went out with some merchants to hunt in the immediate vicinity of the city. Our sport was very poor, but I had an opportunity of seeing the ruins of one of the ancient Indian villages, with its mound, like a natural hill, in the centre. The remains of houses, enclosures, irrigating streams, and burial-mounds, scattered over this plain, cannot fail to give one a high idea of the condition and number of the ancient population. When their earthenware, woollen clothes, utensils of elegant forms (cut out of the hardest rocks), tools of copper, ornaments of precious stones, palaces, and water-works are considered, it is impossible not to respect the considerable advance made by them in the arts of civilization.

TAHITI.

A CORAL reef encircles the entire line of coast of Tahiti. Within the reef there is an expanse of smooth water, like that of a lake, where the canoes of the natives can ply with safety, and where ships anchor. The lowland, which comes down to the beach of coral-sand, is covered with the most beautiful productions of the intertropical regions. In the midst of bananas, orange, cocoa-nut, and bread-fruit-trees, spots are cleared where yams, sweet potatoes, the sugar-cane and pine-apple are cultivated. Even the brush-wood is an imported fruit-tree, namely,

FRUIT OF THE BREAD-FRUIT-TREE.

AVENUE OF PALMS IN THE BOTANIC GARDENS AT RIO.

the guava, which from its abundance has become as noxious as a weed. In Brazil I have often admired the varied beauty of the bananas, palms, and orange-trees contrasted together; and here we also have the bread-fruit, conspicuous from its large, glossy, and deeply digitated leaf. The little winding paths, cool from the surrounding shade, led to the scattered houses, the owners of which everywhere gave us a cheerful and most hospitable reception. In the case of these beautiful woods, the knowledge of their high productiveness no doubt enters largely into the feeling of admiration.

NEW SOUTH WALES.

Its extreme uniformity is the most remarkable feature in the landscape of the greater part of New South Wales. Everywhere we have an open woodland, the ground being partially covered with a very thin pasture, with little appearance of verdure. The trees nearly all belong to one family, and mostly have their leaves placed in an upright instead of, as in Europe, in a nearly horizontal position: the foliage is scanty, and of a peculiar pale green tint, without any gloss; hence the woods appear light and shadowless. This, although a loss of comfort to the traveller under the scorching rays of summer, is of importance to the farmer, as it allows grass to grow where it otherwise would not. The leaves are not shed periodically; and this appears to be

TAHITIAN COAST SCENERY.

the case in the entire southern hemisphere, namely, South America, Australia, and the Cape of Good Hope. The inhabitants of this hemisphere and of the intertropical regions thus lose, perhaps, one of the most glorious (though to our eyes common) spectacles in the world—the first bursting into full foliage of the leafless tree. They may, however, say that

CAPE TOWN, CAPE OF GOOD HOPE.

we pay dearly for this by having the land covered with mere naked skeletons for so many months. This is too true; but our senses thus gain a keen relish for the exquisite green of the spring, which the eyes of those living within the tropics, sated during the long year with the gorgeous productions of those glowing climates, can never experience. The greater number of the trees, with the exception of some of the blue-gums, do not attain a large size; but they grow tall and tolerably straight, and stand well apart. The bark of some of the *Eucalypti* falls annually, or hangs dead in long shreds, which swing about in the wind, and give to the woods a desolate and untidy appearance. I cannot imagine a more complete contrast, in every respect, than between the forests of Valdivia or Chiloe and the woods of Australia.

West of the Blue Mountains the woodland is generally so open that a person on horseback can gallop through it.

EUCALYPTUS-TREE (BLUE-GUM).

It is traversed by a few flat-bottomed valleys, which are green and free from trees: in such spots the scenery was pretty like that of a park. In the whole country I scarcely saw a place without the marks of a fire; whether these had been more or less recent—whether the stumps were more or less black—was the greatest change which varied the uniformity, so wearisome to the traveller's eye. In these woods there are not many birds. I saw, however, some large flocks of the white cockatoo feeding in a cornfield, and a few of the most beautiful parrots; crows like our English jackdaws were not uncommon, and another bird something like the magpie.

IV.

NATURE.

FORESTS.

SOUTH AMERICA.

AMONG the scenes which are deeply impressed on my mind, none exceed in sublimity the primeval forests, undefaced by the hand of man—whether those of Brazil, where the powers of Life are predominant, or those of Tierra del Fuego, where Death and Decay prevail. Both are temples filled with the varied productions of the God of Nature. No one can stand in these solitudes unmoved, and not feel that there is more in man than the mere breath of his body.

In tropical forests, when quietly walking along the shady pathways, and admiring each successive view, I wished to find language to express my ideas. Epithet after epithet was found too weak to convey to those who have not visited the intertropical regions the sensation of delight which the mind experiences. The land is one great, wild, untidy, luxuriant hot-house, made by Nature for herself, but taken possession of by man, who has studded it with gay houses and formal gardens. How great would be the desire in every admirer of nature to behold, if such were possible, the scenery of another planet! Yet to every person in Europe it may be truly said that, at the distance of only a few degrees from his native soil, the glories of another world are opened to him. In my last walk I stopped again and again to gaze on these beauties, and endeavored to fix in my mind forever an impression which, at the time, I knew must sooner or later fail. The form of the orange-tree, the cocoa-nut, the palm, the mango, the tree-fern, the banana, will remain clear and separate; but the thousand beauties which unite these into one perfect scene must fade away.

MANGO FRUIT.

THE KAURI PINE.

At Waimate, in New Zealand, two missionary gentlemen walked with me to part of a neighboring forest, to show me the famous kauri pine. I measured one of these noble trees and found it thirty-one feet in circumference above the roots. There was another close by, which I did not see, thirty-three feet; and I heard of one no less than forty feet. These trees are remarkable for their smooth cylindrical boles, which run up to a height of sixty, and even ninety, feet, with a nearly equal diameter, and without a single branch. The crown of branches at the top is out of all proportion small to the trunk; and the leaves are likewise small compared with the branches. The forest was here almost composed of the kauri, and the largest trees stood up like gigantic columns of wood.

THE BEECH.

The central part of Tierra del Fuego, where the clay-slate formation occurs, is most favorable to the growth of trees; on the outer coast the poorer granitic soil, and a situation more exposed to the violent winds, do not allow of their attaining any great size. Near Port Famine I have seen more large trees than anywhere else: I measured a winter's-bark which was four feet six inches in girth, and several of the beech were as much as thirteen feet. Captain King also mentions a beech which was seven feet in diameter seventeen feet above the roots.

THE KELP.

There is one marine production which, from its importance, is worthy of a particular history; it is the kelp (or *Macrocystis pyrifera*). This plant grows on every rock, from low-water mark to a great depth, both on the outer coast of Tierra del Fuego and within the channels. I believe, during the voyages of the *Adventure* and *Beagle*, not one rock near the surface was discovered which was not buoyed by this floating weed. The good service it thus affords to vessels navigating near this stormy land is evident; and it certainly has saved many a one from being wrecked. I know few things more surprising than to see this plant growing and flourishing amidst those great breakers of the western ocean, which no mass of rock, let it be ever so hard, can long resist. The stem is round, slimy, and smooth, and seldom has a diameter of so much as an inch. A few taken together are sufficiently strong to support the weight of the large loose stones to

CHRISTMAS HARBOR, KERGUELEN LAND.

which, in the inland channels, they grow attached; and yet some of these stones were so heavy that, when drawn to the surface, they could scarcely be lifted into a boat by one person. Captain Cook, in his second voyage, says that this plant, at Kerguelen Land, rises from a greater depth than twenty-four fathoms; "and as it does not grow in a perpendicular direction, but makes a very acute angle with the bottom, and much of it afterward spreads many fathoms on the surface of the sea, I am well warranted to say that some of it grows to the length of sixty fathoms and upward." I do not suppose the stem of any other plant attains so great a length as three hundred and sixty feet, as stated by Captain Cook. Captain Fitz Roy, moreover, found it growing up from the greater depth of forty-five fathoms. The beds of this sea-weed, even when not of great breadth, make excellent natural floating breakwaters. It is quite curious to see, in an exposed harbor, how soon the waves from the open sea, as they travel through the straggling stems, sink in height and pass into smooth water.

The number of living creatures whose existence intimately depends on the kelp is wonderful. A great volume might be written describing the inhabitants of one of these beds of sea-weed. Almost all the leaves, excepting those that float on the surface, are so thickly incrusted with corallines as to be of a white color. On shaking the great entangled roots, a pile of small fish, shells, cuttle-fish, crabs, sea-eggs, star-fish, etc., all fall out together. Often as I went back to a branch of the kelp, I never failed to discover animals of new and curious structures. I can only compare these great water forests of the southern hemisphere with the land forests in the intertropical regions. Yet, if in any country a forest was destroyed, I do not believe nearly so many species of animals would perish as would here from the destruction of the kelp. Amidst the leaves of this plant numerous species of fish live which nowhere else could find food or shelter; with their destruction the many cormorants and other fishing birds, the ottérs, seals and porpoises would soon perish also; and lastly, the Fuegian savage, the miserable lord of this miserable land, would redouble his cannibal feast, decrease in numbers, and perhaps cease to exist.

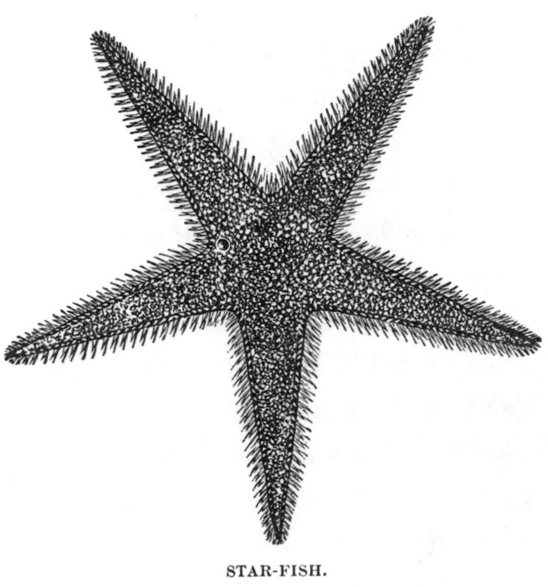

STAR-FISH.

MOUNTAINS.

I WAS frequently surprised, in the scenery of Tierra del Fuego, at the little apparent elevation of mountains really lofty. I suspect it is owing to a cause which would not at first be imagined, namely, that the whole mass, from the summit to the water's edge, is generally in full view. I remember having seen a mountain first from the Beagle Channel, where the whole sweep from the summit to the base was full in view, and then from Ponsonby Sound, across several successive ridges; and it was curious to observe, in the latter case, as each fresh ridge afforded fresh means of judging of the distance, how the mountain rose in height.

Mount Sarmiento is one of the highest in Tierra del Fuego, having an altitude of six thousand eight hundred feet. Its base, for about an eighth of its total height, is clothed by dusky woods, and above this a field of snow extends to the summit. These vast piles of snow, which never melt, and seem destined to last as long as the world holds together, present a noble and even sublime spectacle. Several glaciers descended in a winding course from the upper great expanse of snow to the sea-coast: they may be likened to great frozen Niagaras, and perhaps these cataracts of blue ice are full as beautiful as the moving ones of water.

As the snow-line is so low in Tierra del Fuego, we might have expected that many of the glaciers would have reached the sea. Nevertheless I was astonished when I first saw a range, only from three to four thousand feet in height, with every valley filled with streams of ice descending to the sea-coast. Almost every arm of the sea which penetrates to the inner higher chain, not only in Tierra del Fuego but on the coast for six hundred and fifty miles northward, is terminated by "tremendous and astonishing glaciers," as described by one of the officers of the survey. Great masses of ice frequently fall from these icy cliffs, and the crash re-echoes, like the broadside of a man-of-war, through the lonely channels. It is known that earthquakes frequently cause masses of earth to fall from sea-cliffs; how terrific, then, would be the effect of a severe shock (and such do occur here) on a body like a glacier, already in motion and traversed by fissures! I can readily believe that the water would be fairly beaten back out of the deepest channel, and then, returning with an overwhelming force, would whirl about huge masses of rock like so much chaff. In Eyre's Sound, in a (south) latitude corresponding with that of Paris, there are immense glaciers, and yet the loftiest neighboring mountain is only six thousand two hundred feet high. In this sound about fifty icebergs were seen at one time floating outward, and one of them must have been *at least* one hundred and sixty-eight feet in total height. Some of the icebergs were loaded with blocks, of no inconsiderable size, of granite and other rocks, different from the clay-slate of the surrounding mountains. The glacier farthest from the Pole, surveyed during the voyages of the *Adventure* and *Beagle*, is in latitude 46° 50′, in the Gulf of Peñas. It is fifteen miles long, and in one part seven broad, and descends to the sea-coast.

From the east coast of the island of Chiloe, on a splendidly clear day (November 26, 1834), we saw the volcano of Osorno spouting out volumes of smoke. This most beautiful mountain, formed like a perfect cone, and white with snow, stands out in front of the Cordillera. Another great volcano, with a saddle-shaped summit, also emitted from its immense crater little jets of steam. Afterward we saw the lofty-peaked Corcovado (Hunchback)—well deserving the name of "famous" (*el famoso Corcovado*). Thus we beheld, from one point of view, three great active volcanoes, each about seven thousand feet high. In addition to this, far to the south, there were other lofty cones covered with snow, which, although not known to be active, must be in their origin volcanic. The line of the Andes is not, in this neighborhood, nearly so elevated as in Chile; neither does it appear to form so perfect a barrier between the regions of the earth. This great range, although running in a straight north and south line, always appeared more or less curved.

FOSSIL TREES.

In the central part of the Uspallata range, at an elevation of about seven thousand feet, I observed on a bare slope some snow-white projecting columns. These were petrified fir-trees, abruptly broken off, the upright stumps projecting a few feet above the ground. The trunks, some fifty in number, measured from three to five feet each in circumference. They stood a little way apart from each other, but the whole formed one group. I confess I was at first so much astonished that I could scarcely believe the marvellous story which this scene at once unfolded. I saw the spot where a cluster of fine trees once waved their branches on the shores of the Atlantic, when that ocean (now driven back seven hundred miles) came to the foot of the Andes. I saw that they had sprung from a volcanic soil, which had been raised above the level of the sea, and that afterward this dry land, with its upright trees, had been let down into the depths of the ocean. In these depths the formerly dry land was covered by beds of sediment, and these again by enormous streams of submarine lava—one such mass attaining the thickness of a thousand feet; and these deluges of molten

USPALLATA PASS.

stone and watery deposits five times alternately had been spread out. The ocean which received such thick masses must have been profoundly deep; but again the subterranean forces exerted themselves, and I now beheld the bed of that ocean forming a chain of mountains more than seven thousand feet in height. Nor had those opposing forces been idle which are always at work wearing down the surface of the land: the great piles of strata had been cut through by many wide valleys, and the trees, now changed into silex, were exposed projecting from the volcanic soil (now changed into rock), whence formerly, in a green and budding state, they had raised their lofty heads. Now all is utterly irreclaimable and desert; even the lichen cannot cling to the stony casts of former trees. Vast and scarcely comprehensible as such changes must ever appear, yet they have all occurred within a period which is recent when compared with the history of the Cordillera; and the Cordillera itself is absolutely modern as compared with many of the fossiliferous strata of Europe and America.

In the valley of Copiapó, in northern Chile, I stayed two days collecting fossil shells and wood. Great prostrate silicified trunks of trees were extraordinarily numerous. I measured one which was fifteen feet in circumference. How surprising it is that every atom of the woody matter in this great cylinder should have been removed, and replaced by silex so perfectly that each vessel and pore is preserved! These trees all belonged to the fir-tribe. It was amusing to hear the inhabitants discussing the nature of the fossil shells which I collected, almost in the same terms as were used a century ago in Europe, namely, whether or not they had been thus "born by nature."

AN OLD SEA-BED.

THE landscape has a uniform character from the Strait of Magellan along the whole eastern coast of Patagonia to the Rio Colorado; and it appears that the same kind of country extends inland from this river in a sweeping line

CAPE FROWARD (PATAGONIA), STRAIT OF MAGELLAN.

as far as San Luis, and perhaps even farther north. To the eastward of this curved line lies the basin of the comparatively damp and green plains of Buenos Ayres. The sterile plains of Mendoza and Patagonia consist of a bed of shingle, worn smooth, and accumulated by the waves of the sea;

while the Pampas, covered by thistles, clover and grass, have been formed by the ancient estuary mud of the Plata.

EARTHQUAKES.

This day (Febuary 20, 1835) has been memorable, in the annals of Valdivia, for the most severe earthquake experienced by the oldest inhabitant. I happened to be on shore, and was lying down in the wood to rest myself. It came on suddenly, and lasted two minutes, but the time appeared much longer. The rocking of the ground was very sensible. There was no difficulty in standing upright, but the motion made me almost giddy; it was something like the movement of a vessel in a cross-ripple, or still more like that felt by a person skating over thin ice, which bends under the weight of his body.

A bad earthquake at once destroys our oldest associations: the earth, the very emblem of solidity, has moved beneath our feet like a thin crust over a fluid; one second of time has created in the mind a strange idea of insecurity which hours of reflection would not have produced. In the forest, as a breeze moved the trees, I felt only the earth tremble, but saw no other effect. Captain Fitz Roy and some officers were at the town during the shock, and there the scene was more striking; for although the houses, from being built of wood, did not fall, they were violently shaken, and the boards creaked and rattled together. The people rushed out-of-doors in the greatest alarm. The tides were very curiously affected. The great shock took place at the time of low-water, and an old woman who was on the beach told me that the water flowed very quickly (but not in great waves) to high-water mark, and then as quickly returned to its proper level; this was also evident by the line of wet sand.

On the fourth of March we entered the harbor of Concepcion. While the ship was beating up to the anchorage I landed on the island of Quiriquina. The mayor-domo of the estate quickly rode down to tell me the terrible news of the great earthquake of the 20th: "That not a house in Concepcion or Talcahuano (the port) was standing; that seventy villages were destroyed; and that a great wave had almost washed away the ruins of Talcahuano." Of this latter statement I soon saw abundant proofs, the whole coast being strewed over with timber and furniture, as if a thousand ships had been wrecked. Besides chairs, tables, book-shelves, etc., in great numbers, there were several roofs of cottages, which had been transported almost whole. The storehouses at Talcahuano had been burst open, and great bags of cotton, yerba, and other valuable merchandise, were scattered on the shore. During my walk around the island I observed that numerous fragments of rock, which, from the marine productions adhering to them, must recently have been lying in deep water, had been cast up high on the beach; one of these was six feet long, three broad and thick. I believe this convulsion has done more to lessen the size of the island of Quiriquina than the ordinary wear-and-tear of the sea and weather during the course of a whole century.

The next day I landed at Talcahuano, and afterward rode to Concepcion. Both towns presented the most awful yet interesting spectacle I ever beheld. To the person who had formerly known them it might possibly have been still more impressive; for the ruins were so mingled together, and the whole scene possessed so little the air of a habitable place, that it was scarcely possible to imagine its former condition. The earthquake commenced at half-past eleven o'clock in the forenoon. If it had happened in the middle of the night the greater number of the inhabitants (which in this one province amounts to many thousands) must have perished, instead of less than a hundred: as it was, the invariable practice of running out of doors at the first trembling of the ground, alone saved them. In Concepcion each house, or row of houses, stood by itself, a heap or line of ruins; but in Talcahuano, owing to the great wave, little more than one layer of bricks, tiles, and timber, with here and there part of a wall left standing, could be distinguished. From this circumstance Concepcion, although not so completely desolated, was a more terrible, and, if I may so call it, picturesque sight. The first shock was very sudden. The mayor-domo at Quiriquina told me that the first notice he received of it was finding both the horse he rode and himself rolling together on the ground. Rising up, he was again thrown down. He also told me that some cows which were standing on the steep side of the island were rolled into the sea. The great wave caused the destruction of many cattle; on one low island, near the head of the bay, seventy animals were washed off and drowned. Innumerable small tremblings followed the great earthquake, and within the first twelve days no less than three hundred were counted.

After viewing Concepcion, I cannot understand how the greater number of inhabitants escaped unhurt. The houses in many parts fell outward, thus forming in the middle of the streets little hillocks of brickwork and rubbish. Mr. Rouse, the English consul, told us that he was at breakfast when the first movement warned him to run out. He had scarcely reached the middle of the court-yard when one side of his house came thundering down. He had presence of mind to remember that if he once got on the top of that part which had already fallen, he would be safe. Not being able, from the motion of the ground, to stand, he crawled upon his hands and knees; and no sooner had he ascended this little eminence than the other side of the house fell in, the great beams sweeping close in front of his head. With his eyes blinded, and his mouth choked with the cloud of dust which darkened the sky, at last he gained the street. As shock followed shock, at the interval of a few minutes, no one dared approach the shattered ruins, and no one knew whether his dearest friends and relations were not perishing from the want of help. Those who had saved any property were obliged to keep a constant watch, for thieves prowled about, and, at each little trembling of the ground, with one hand they beat their breasts and cried mercy (*misericordia*), and then with the other filched what they could from the ruins! The thatched roofs fell over the fires, and flames burst forth in all parts. Hundreds knew themselves ruined, and few had the means of providing food for the day. Generally speaking, arched door-ways or windows stood much better than any other parts of buildings. Nevertheless, a poor lame old man, who had been in the habit, during trifling shocks, of crawling to a certain door-way, was this time crushed to pieces.

Shortly after the shock a great wave was seen from the distance of three or four miles, approaching in the middle of the bay with a smooth outline; but along the shore it tore up cottages and trees as it swept onward with irresistible force. At the head of the bay it broke in a fearful line of white breakers, which rushed up to a height of twenty-three vertical feet above the highest spring-tides. Their force must have been prodigious, for at the fort a cannon with its carriage, estimated at four tons in weight, was moved fifteen feet inward. A schooner was left in the midst of the ruins, two hundred yards from the beach. The first wave was followed by two others, which in their retreat carried away a vast wreck of floating objects. In one part of the bay a ship was pitched high and dry on shore, was carried off, again driven on shore, and again carried off. In another part, two large vessels anchored near together were whirled about, and their cables were thrice wound round each other: though anchored at a depth of thirty-six feet, they were for some minutes aground. The great wave must have travelled slowly, for the inhabitants of Talcahuano had time to run up the hills behind the town; and some sailors pulled out seaward, trusting successfully to their boat riding securely over the swell if they could reach it before it broke. One old woman, with a little boy four or five years old, ran into a boat, but there was nobody to row it out—the boat was consequently dashed against an anchor and cut in twain; the old woman was drowned, but the child was picked up some hours afterward clinging to the wreck. Pools of salt-water were still standing amidst the ruins of the houses; and children, making boats with old tables and chairs, appeared as happy as their parents were miserable. It was, however, exceedingly interesting to observe how much more active and cheerful all appeared than could have been expected. Mr. Rouse, and a large party whom he kindly took under his protection, lived for the first week in a garden beneath some apple-trees. At first they were as merry as if it had been a picnic; but soon afterward heavy rain caused much discomfort, for they were absolutely without shelter.

The common people in Talcahuano thought that the earthquake was caused by some old Indian women who, two years ago, being offended, stopped the volcano of Antuco. This silly belief is curious, because it shows that experience has taught them to observe that there exists a relation between the suppressed action of the volcanoes and the trembling of the ground; and particularly because in this instance, according to Captain Fitz Roy, there is reason to believe that Antuco was noway affected. The island of Juan Fernandez, three hundred and sixty miles to the north-west, was, at the time of the great shock of the 20th, violently shaken, so that the trees beat against each other, and a volcano burst forth under water close to the shore. These facts are remarkable, because this island, during the earthquake of 1751, was then also affected more violently than other places at an equal distance from Concepcion, and this seems to show some subterranean connection between these two points.

Chiloe, about three hundred and forty miles southward of Concepcion, appears to have been shaken more strongly than

ISLAND OF JUAN FERNANDEZ (ROBINSON CRUSOE'S).

the intermediate district of Valdivia, where the volcano of Villarica was noway affected, while in the Cordillera in front of Chiloe two of the volcanoes burst forth at the same instant in violent action. These two volcanoes and some neighboring ones continued for a long time in eruption, and ten months afterward were again influenced by an earthquake at Concepcion. Some men, cutting wood near the base of one of these volcanoes, did not perceive the shock of the 20th, although the whole surrounding province was then

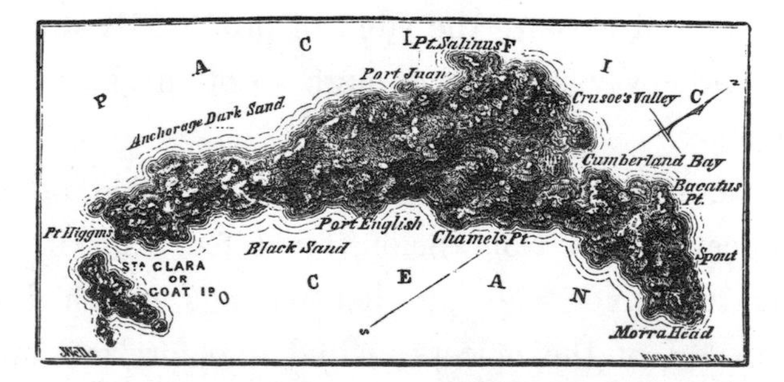

MAP OF THE ISLAND OF JUAN FERNANDEZ.

trembling. Here we have an eruption relieving and taking the place of an earthquake, as would have happened at Concepcion, according to the belief of the common people, if the volcano of Antuco had not been closed by witchcraft. Two years and three-quarters afterward Valdivia and Chiloe were again shaken, more violently than on the 20th, and an island in the Chonos Archipelago was permanently raised more than eight feet. We may, therefore, confidently come to the conclusion that the forces which, slowly and by little starts, uplift continents, and those which at successive periods pour forth volcanic matter from open orifices, are the same.

CRUSOE.

It is remarkable that while Talcahuano and Callao (near Lima), both situated at the head of large shallow bays, have suffered during every severe earthquake from great waves, Valparaiso, seated close to the edge of profoundly deep water, has never been overwhelmed, though so often shaken by the severest shocks.

I have not attempted to give any detailed description of the appearance of Concepcion, for I feel that it is quite impossible to convey the mingled feelings which I experienced. Several of the officers visited it before me, but their strongest language failed to give a just idea of the scene of desolation. It is a bitter and humiliating thing to see works which have cost man so much time and labor overthrown in one minute; yet compassion for the inhabitants was almost instantly banished by the surprise in seeing a state of things produced in a moment of time which one was accustomed to attribute to a succession of ages. In my opinion, we have scarcely beheld, since leaving England, any sight so deeply interesting.

Earthquakes alone are sufficient to destroy the prosperity of any country. If beneath England the now inert subterranean forces should exert those powers which most assuredly in former geological ages they have exerted, how completely would the entire condition of the country be changed! What would become of the lofty houses, thickly packed cities, great manufactories, the beautiful public and private edifices? If the new period of disturbance were first to commence by some great earthquake in the dead of the night, how terrific would be the carnage! England would at once become bankrupt; all papers, records, and accounts would from that moment be lost. Government being unable to collect the taxes, and failing to maintain its authority, the hand of violence and rapine would remain uncontrolled. In every large town famine would go forth, pestilence and death following in its train!

On the 14th of May we reached Coquimbo, and in the evening Captain Fitz Roy and myself were dining with Mr. Edwards, an English resident, when a short earthquake happened. I heard the forthcoming rumble; but, from the screams of the ladies, the running of the servants, and the rush of several of the gentlemen to the doorway, I could not distinguish the motion. Some of the women afterward were crying with terror, and one gentleman said he should not be able to sleep all night, or if he did, it would only be to dream of falling houses. The father of this person had lately lost all his property at Talcahuano, and he himself had only just escaped a falling roof at Valparaiso, in 1822. He mentioned a curious coincidence which then happened: he was playing at cards, when a German, one of the party, got up, and said he would never sit in a room in these countries with the door shut, as, owing to his having done so, he had nearly lost his life at Copiapó. Accordingly he opened the door, and no sooner had he done this than he cried out, "Here it comes again!" and the famous shock commenced. The whole party escaped. The danger in an earthquake is not from the time lost in opening a door, but from the chance of its being jammed by the movement of the walls.

It is impossible to be much surprised at the fear which natives and old residents, though some of them known to be men of great command of mind, so generally experience during earthquakes. I think, however, this excess of panic may be partly attributed to a want of habit in governing their fear, as it is not a feeling they are ashamed of. Indeed, the natives do not like to see a person indifferent. I heard of two Englishmen who, sleeping in the open air during a smart shock, knowing that there was no danger, did not rise. The natives cried out indignantly, "Look at those heretics; they will not even get out of their beds!"

RAINFALL.

As we travelled north, along the coast from Valparaiso, (May, 1835), the country became more and more barren. In the valleys there was scarcely water enough for any irrigation, and the intermediate land was quite bare, not supporting even goats. In the spring, after the winter showers, a thin pasture rapidly springs up, and cattle are then driven down from the Cordillera to graze for a short time. It is curious to observe how the seeds of the grass and other plants seem to accommodate themselves, as if by habit, to the quantity of rain which falls on different parts of this coast. One shower far northward at Copiapó produces as great an effect on the vegetation as two at Guasco, and as three or four in the Conchalee district. At Valparaiso a winter so dry as greatly to injure the pasture would, at Guasco, produce the most unusual abundance. At Conchalee, which is only sixty-seven miles north of Valparaiso, rain is not expected until the end of May; whereas, at Valparaiso, some generally falls early in April.

On the morning of the 17th of May, at Coquimbo, it rained lightly, the first time this year, for about five hours. The farmers, who plant corn near the sea-coast, where the atmosphere is moister, taking advantage of this shower, would break up the ground; after a second, they would put the seed in; and if a third shower should fall, they would reap a good harvest in the spring. It was interesting to watch the effect of this trifling amount of moisture. Twelve hours afterward the ground appeared as dry as ever; yet after an interval of ten days all the hills were faintly tinged with green patches, the grass being sparingly scattered in hair-like fibres a full inch in length. Before this shower every part of the surface was bare as on a high-road. The epithets "barren" and "sterile" are certainly applicable to northern Chile, yet even here there are not many spaces of two hundred yards square where some little bush, cactus, or lichen may not be discovered by careful examination; and in the soil seeds lie dormant, ready to spring up during the first rainy winter.

In the valley of Copiapó the small quantity of cultivated land does not so much depend on inequalities of level and consequent unfitness for irrigation, as on the small supply of water. The river this year was remarkably full: high up in the valley it reached to the horses' bellies, and was about fifteen yards wide, and rapid; lower down it becomes smaller and smaller, and is generally quite lost, as happened during one period of thirty years, so that not a drop entered the sea. The inhabitants watch a storm over the Cordillera with great interest, as one good fall of snow provides them with water for the ensuing year. This is of infinitely more consequence than rain in the lower country. Rain, as often as it falls—which is about once in every two or three years—is a great advantage, because the cattle and mules can for some time afterward find a little pasture on the mountains. But without snow on the Andes, desolation extends throughout the valley. It is on record that three times nearly all the inhabitants have been obliged to emigrate to the south. This year there was plenty of water, and every man irrigated his ground as much as he chose; but it has frequently been necessary to post soldiers at the sluices, to see that each estate took only its proper allowance during so many hours in the week.

HIBERNATION OF ANIMALS.

When we first arrived at Bahia Blanca, September 7th, 1832, we thought nature had granted scarcely a living creature to this sandy and dry country. By digging, however, in the ground, several insects, large spiders, and lizards were found in a half-torpid state. On the 15th, a few animals began to appear, and by the 18th (three days from the equinox), everything announced the commencement of spring. The plains were ornamented by the flowers of a pink wood-sorrel, wild pease, and geraniums; and the birds began to lay their eggs. Numerous insects were crawling slowly about; while the lizard tribe, the constant inhabitants of a sandy soil, darted about in every direction. During the first eleven days, while nature was dormant, the average temperature was 51°; and in the middle of the day the thermometer seldom ranged above 55°. On the eleven succeeding days, in which all living things became so animated, the average was 58°, and the range in the middle of the day between 60° and 70°. Here, then, an increase of seven degrees in the average temperature, but a greater one of extreme heat, was sufficient to awaken the functions of life. At Montevideo, from which we had just before sailed, in the twenty-three days included between the 26th of July and the 19th of August, the average temperature was 58.4°, the average hottest day being 65.5°, and the coldest 46°. The lowest point to which the thermometer fell was 41.5°, and occasionally in the middle of the day it rose to 69° or 70°. Yet with this high temperature, almost every beetle, several genera of spiders, snails, and land-shells, toads and lizards, were all lying torpid beneath stones. But we have seen that at Bahia Blanca, which is four degrees southward, and therefore has a climate only a very little colder, this same temperature, with a rather less extreme heat, was sufficient to awake all orders of animated beings. This shows how nicely the arousing of hibernating animals is governed by the usual climate of the district, and not by the absolute heat.

THE OCEAN.

WHAT are the boasted glories of the illimitable ocean? A tedious waste, a desert of water, as the Arabian calls it. No doubt there are some delightful scenes: a moonlight night, with the clear heavens and the dark glittering sea, and the white sails filled by the soft air of a gently-blowing trade-wind; a dead calm, with the heaving surface polished like a mirror, and all still except the occasional flapping of the canvas. It is well once to behold a squall with its rising arch and coming fury, or the heavy gale of wind and mountainous waves. I confess, however, my imagination had painted something more grand, more terrific in the full-grown storm. It is an incomparably finer spectacle when beheld on shore, where the waving trees, the wild flight of the birds, the dark shadows and bright lights, the rushing of the torrents, all proclaim the strife of the unloosed elements. At sea the albatross and little petrel fly as if the storm were their proper sphere, the water rises and sinks as if fulfilling its usual task; the ship alone and its inhabitants seem the objects of wrath. On a forlorn and weather-beaten coast the scene is indeed different, but the feelings partake more of horror than of wild delight.

THE ALBATROSS.

It is necessary to sail over the Pacific to comprehend its immensity. Moving quickly onward for weeks together, we meet with nothing but the same blue, profoundly deep ocean. Even within the archipelagoes the islands are mere specks, and far distant one from the other. Accustomed to look at maps drawn on a small scale, where dots, shading, and names are crowded together, we do not rightly judge how infinitely small the proportion of dry land is to the water of this vast expanse.

LAGOON ISLANDS.

On the first of April, 1836, we arrived in view of the Keeling or Cocos Islands, situated in the Indian Ocean, and about six hundred miles distant from the coast of Sumatra.

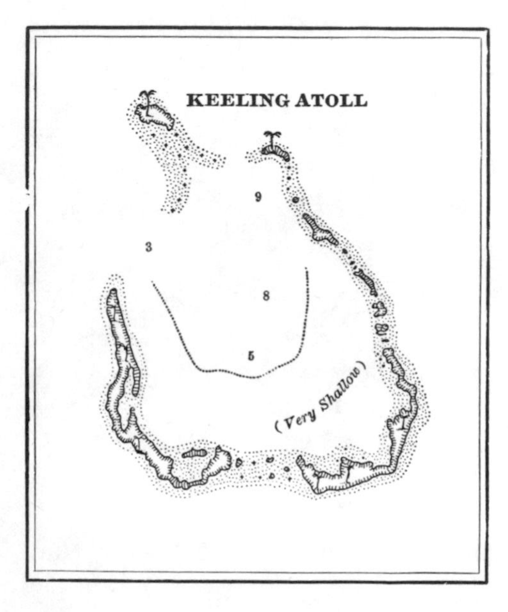

This is one of the lagoon islands (or atolls) of coral formation. Its ring-formed reef is surmounted in the greater part of its length by narrow islets. On the northern or leeward side there is an opening through which vessels can pass to the anchorage within—the shallow, clear, and still water of the lagoon, which, resting in its greater part on white sand, is, when illumined by a vertical sun, of the most vivid green.

On the 6th I accompanied Captain Fitz Roy to an island at the head of the lagoon. The channel was exceedingly intricate, winding through fields of delicately branched corals. When we arrived at the head, we crossed a narrow islet, and found a great surf breaking on the windward coast. I can hardly explain the reason, but there is to my mind much grandeur in the view of the outer shores of these lagoon islands. There is a simplicity in the barrier-like beach, the margin of green bushes and tall cocoa-nuts, the solid flat of dead coral-rock, strewed here and there with great loose fragments, and the line of furious breakers, all rounding away toward either hand. The ocean, throwing its waters over the broad reef, appears an invincible, all-powerful enemy; yet we see it resisted and even conquered by means which at first seem most weak and inefficient. It is not that the ocean spares the rock of coral: the great fragments scattered over the reef, and heaped on the beach, whence the tall cocoa-nut springs, plainly bespeak the unrelenting power of the waves. Nor are any periods of repose granted. The long swell caused by the gentle but steady action of the trade-wind, always blowing in one direction over a wide area, causes breakers almost equalling in force those during a gale of wind in the temperate regions, and which never cease to rage. It is impossible to behold these waves without feeling a con-

VIEW OF AN ATOLL.

viction that an island, though built of the hardest rock, let it be porphyry, granite, or quartz, would ultimately yield, and be demolished by such an irresistible power. Yet these low, insignificant coral islets stand and are victorious; for here another power, as an antagonist, takes part in the contest.

The living polyps separate the atoms of carbonate of lime, one by one, from the foaming breakers, and unite them into a symmetrical structure. Let the hurricane tear up its thousand huge fragments; yet what will that tell against the accumulated labor of myriads of architects at work night and day, month after month? Thus do we see the soft and gelati-

COCOA-NUT PALM.

nous body of a polypus, through the agency of the vital laws, conquering the great mechanical power of the waves of an ocean which neither the art of man nor the inanimate works of nature could successfully resist.

A few miles north of Keeling there is another small atoll, the lagoon of which is nearly filled up with coral mud. Cap-

CORAL ARCHITECTS.

ADELBERT VON CHAMISSO.

tain Ross found embedded in the conglomerate on the outer coast a well-moulded fragment of greenstone, rather larger than a man's head. He and the men with him were so much surprised at this that they brought it away and preserved it as a curiosity. The occurrence of this one stone, where every other particle of matter is of lime, certainly is very puzzling. The island has scarcely ever been visited, nor is it probable that a ship had been wrecked there. From the absence of any better explanation, I came to the conclusion that it must have become entangled in the roots of some large tree; when, however, I considered the great distance from the nearest land, the combination of chances against a stone thus being entangled, the tree washed into the sea, floated so far, then landed safely, and the stone finally so embedded as to allow of its discovery, I was almost afraid of imagining a means of transport apparently so improbable. It was, therefore, with great interest that I found Chamisso, the justly distinguished naturalist who accompanied Kotzebue, stating that the inhabitants of the Radack Archipelago (a group of lagoon islands in the midst of the Pacific) obtained stones for sharpening their instruments by searching the roots of trees which are cast upon the beach. It will be evident that this must have happened several times, since laws have been established that such stones belong to the chief, and a punishment is inflicted on any one who attempts to steal them.

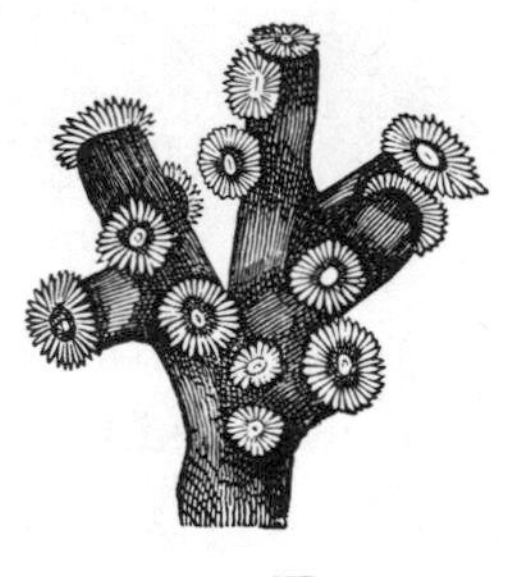

A POLYP.

In the morning of April 12th we stood out of the lagoon

on our passage to the Isle of France. I am glad we have visited these islands: such formations surely rank high among the wonderful objects of this world. Captain Fitz Roy found no bottom with a line seven thousand two hundred feet in length, at the distance of only two thousand two hundred

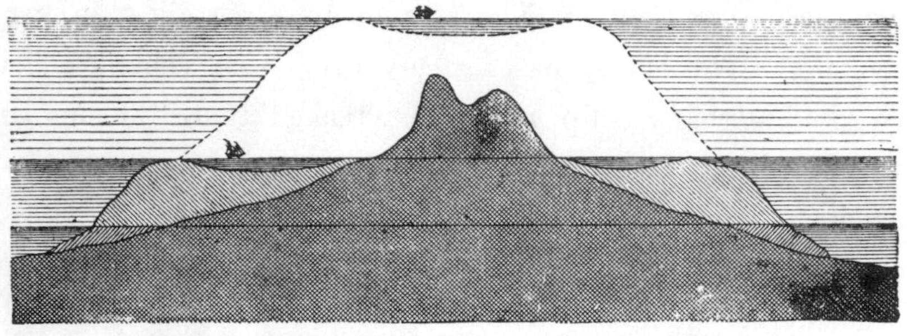

GROWTH OF CORAL ON A MOUNTAIN SLOWLY SUBSIDING.

yards from the shore; hence this island forms a lofty submarine mountain, with sides steeper even than those of the most abrupt volcanic cone. The saucer-shaped summit is nearly ten miles across; and every single atom, from the least particle to the largest fragment of rock in this great pile (which, however, is small compared with very many lagoon islands), bears the stamp of having been subjected to organic arrangement. We feel surprised when travellers tell us of the vast dimensions of the Pyramids and other great ruins; but how utterly insignificant are the greatest of these when compared to these mountains of stone, accumulated by the agency of various minute and tender animals! This is a wonder which does not at first strike the eye of the body but, after reflection, the eye of reason.

INDEX

OF NAMES OF NOTABLE PERSONS MENTIONED IN THE FOREGOING PAGES.

JOHN J. AUDUBON.

INDEX

OF NAMES OF PERSONS MENTIONED IN THE FOREGOING PAGES.

Audubon, JOHN JAMES. (Page 69.) An American ornithologist, born of French parents in Louisiana, May 4th, 1780; died in New York city, January 27th, 1851. His great work, "The Birds of America," began to be published in 1826, and was thirteen years in reaching completion. He himself furnished the colored drawings from which the copperplates, upward of four hundred in number, were engraved. Some of these plates are exhibited at the New York Museum of Natural History in Central Park. His account of the carrion-crows or black vultures, to which Mr. Darwin refers, is given in Audubon's "Ornithological Biography" (vol. ii., p. 33), published in 1831–49.

Bonpland, AIMÉ. (Page 145.) A French botanist; born at La Rochelle, August 22d, 1773; died May 4th, 1858, at Santa Anna, in the Argentine Province of Corrientes. He accompanied Humboldt in his journey to South America in 1799. In 1816 he went again to that country, and lived by turns in La Plata (now the Argentine Confederation), Uruguay, Paraguay (at first as a prisoner of war), and Brazil. He was unwilling to return to Europe.

Burchell, WILLIAM J. (Page 73.) An English traveller. His "Travels in the Interior of Southern Africa" was published in London in 1822–24.

Byron, JOHN. (Page 44.) An English naval commander; born November 8th, 1723; died April 10th, 1786: the grandfather of Lord

ADMIRAL JOHN BYRON.

Byron, the poet. He accompanied Anson in his voyage round the world, leaving England in September, 1740. In May, 1741, he was shipwrecked on the west coast of Patagonia. The great hardships which he suffered in consequence of this he afterward related in his "Narrative of the Honorable John Byron (Commodore in a late Expedition Round the World), containing an Account of the great Distresses suffered by Himself and his Companions on the Coast of Patagonia, from the year 1740 till their Arrival in England, 1746" (London, 1768). The "late expedition" referred to in this title took place in 1764–66.

Chamisso, ADELBERT. (Page 203.) A poet and naturalist; born of French parentage at Boncourt, in Champagne, France, January 27th, 1781; died in Berlin, August 21st, 1838. At an early age he removed with his parents to Berlin, where he was educated, and entered the Prussian military service. His writings, consequently, were in German. In 1815–18 he accompanied Kotzebue in the Romanoff expedition round the world, and besides furnishing part of the Report which appeared in 1821, wrote a separate account, first published in 1836–39. He is best known to English readers as the author of the remarkable story called "Peter Schlemihl"—the man who parted with his shadow.

CAPTAIN JAMES COOK.

Cook, James. (Pp. 94, 174.) An English navigator; born October 27th, 1728, in Yorkshire; killed by the Sandwich Islanders February 14th, 1779. As master of the sloop *Mercury* he assisted in the taking of Quebec by Wolfe, in 1759. His first voyage to the southern hemisphere was in the employ of the Government, beginning in 1768. He visited Tahiti and New Zealand, and explored the east coast of Australia, as Dampier had done the west. He returned to England

KARAKAKOOA BAY, THE SCENE OF CAPTAIN COOK'S DEATH.

in 1771, and was sent out the following year, in command of the *Resolution*, in search of the Antarctic continent. On this voyage he discovered New Caledonia, and returned to England in 1775. Captain Cook's third voyage was undertaken in 1776, for the sake of a reward offered by Parliament to the discoverer of a northern passage from the Pacific to the Atlantic. He discovered the Sandwich Islands in January, 1778, afterward explored Behring Strait, and on sailing homeward stopped again at the islands. The natives of

Hawaii showed themselves unfriendly, and a quarrel having arisen during a landing, they fell upon Cook and his men, and the great captain was slain. The Journal of Captain Cook's second voyage (the one referred to by Mr. Darwin) was published in London in 1777; the Journal of the last voyage, in 1781.

Cowley, Captain. (Page 77.) An English navigator, who, as did also Captain William Dampier, accompanied Captain John Cooke in a voyage round the world in 1683–84. In the year first named Cowley happened to be in Virginia, and was prevailed upon by Cooke to go as sailing-master of his ship *Revenge*, on a trading voyage to Hàyti. Cooke, however, was really a buccaneer, and the story was only a pretence. They sailed, then, August 23d, 1683, for the South Seas, by way of the African coast (where they captured a new and better-armed ship, to which they transferred themselves and the name of their old ship), Brazil, the Falkland Islands, Tierra del Fuego, the island of Juan Fernandez, the Lobos Islands west of Peru, Panama, and the Galapagos (*i. e.*, Turtle) Islands, which were sighted May 31st, 1684. A month later Cooke died, and, in September, Cowley left the *Revenge* to sail the *Nicholas*, another pirate ship, with which they had kept company after rounding Cape Horn. His course now lay to the Asiatic coast and archipelago. At Timor, in December, 1685, Cowley quitted the *Nicholas* and went to Batavia, where, in the following March, he embarked for Holland, and reached London October 12th, 1686. This account of him will be found in Robert Kerr's "General History and Collection of Voyages and Travels" (Edinburgh, 1814).

Dampier, William. (Page 77.) An English navigator: born 1652, in Somersetshire; the year of his death is unknown, but it was later than 1711. He had a most adventurous life on sea and on land in both hemispheres. In July, 1682, after a season of buccaneering, he arrived in Virginia, and in the following year fell in with Captain John Cooke, a native of St. Kitts, in the West Indies, and joined him (with less compunction than did Captain Cowley) in his piratical expedition. He remained by the *Revenge* when Cowley left it, and cruised about the Pacific, both on the American coast and in the East Indies, till May 4th, 1688, when, wearying of his wretched mode of life, he abandoned it at the Nicobar Islands and arrived at Atcheen,

CAPTAIN WILLIAM DAMPIER.

in Sumatra, in June. He afterward went to Tonquin, and returned to Atcheen in April, 1689. On January 25th, 1691, he set sail for England, and reached London September 16th, after an absence of twelve and a half years. He told his marvellous story in a book called a "New Voyage Round the World," published in London in 1697. Being then taken into the English service, and put in command of the *Roebuck*, he sailed in 1699, on behalf of the Government, to the Southern Ocean, exploring the coasts of Australia and New Guinea, and discovering many unknown lands. On his homeward voyage he was shipwrecked on Ascension Island in February, 1701, but reached London the same year and again told his story in a book. He made at least two more voyages—with Captain William Funnell, 1703–05, and with Captains Woods Rogers and Stephen Courtney, 1708–11—for the plundering of Spanish ships in the South Sea. On the latter voyage Alexander Selkirk (the original Robinson Crusoe) was found on the island of Juan Fernandez and taken on board as one of the mates.

Falconer, RICHARD. (Page 46.) An English navigator; author of a work describing his "Voyages, Dangerous Adventures, and Imminent Escapes" (London, 1724).

Fitz Roy, ROBERT. (Pp. 102, 105, 151, 174, 183, 188, 191, 198, 204.) An English navigator and meteorologist; born July 5th, 1805; died April 30th, 1865. He entered the navy in 1819, and in 1828 was associated with Captain King in an exploring expedition to the coasts of Patagonia and Chile. In 1831 he commanded the *Beagle* in the expedition round the world which Mr. Darwin accompanied as naturalist. The results of both these voyages were published under the title, "Narrative of the Surveying Voyages of H.M.SS. *Adventure* and *Beagle*, 1826–1836" (London, 1839). Captain Fitz Roy was afterward Governor of New Zealand. His last years were devoted to meteorological study and observations.

Gould, JOHN. (Page 50.) An English ornithologist; born September 14th, 1804, at Lyme-Regis, in Dorsetshire, England, and still living (1879). His first published work, "A Century of Birds from the Himalaya Mountains," appeared in 1832; his second, "The Birds of Europe," in 1832–37. The next two years were spent in travels in Australia, which led to two other important publications,

"The Mammals of Australia" (1845), and "The Birds of Australia" (1848–1869). He is also the author of a "Hand-book to the Birds of Australia" (1865), and "The Birds of Great Britain" (1862–1873). Mr. Gould contributed the chapter on birds in the zoological report of the voyage of the *Beagle.*

Head, Francis Bond. (Page 130.) A British officer; born near Rochester, Kent, England, in 1793; died July, 1869. While an army captain he went to South America in 1825, as agent of a mining association, and in 1826 published "Rough Notes taken during some Rapid Journeys across the Pampas and among the Andes," of which Mr. Darwin praises the "spirit and accuracy." In 1836 he was Lieutenant-Governor of Canada.

King, Philip Parker. (Pp. 72, 172.) A British naval commander; born in the island of Norfolk, South Pacific Ocean, in 1793. In 1817–22 he was engaged in completing the survey of the west coast of Australia. In 1826 he commanded the expedition sent out to explore the coasts of South America, his ship being the *Adventure.* His survey and that of the *Beagle* were published together. (See Fitz Roy, above.)

Kotzebue, Otto von. (Page 203.) Born at Reval, in Russia, of German parents, in 1787; died there in 1846. He accompanied Admiral von Krusenstern in his voyage around the world in 1803–6, and in 1815–18, in the ship *Rurick,* again made the voyage as chief, accompanied by Chamisso (see above) and others. Out of this came his "Voyage of Discovery into the South Sea and Behring's Straits, for the purpose of Exploring a Northeast Passage" (London, 1821). He made a third and last voyage in 1823–26, of which he gave an account in his "New Voyage Around the World" (London, 1830).

Pernety, Antoine Joseph. (Page 80.) Born at Roanne, France, in 1716; died in 1801. He was for some time librarian of Frederic the Great. His "Voyage to the Falkland Islands" was published in 1769.

Rosas, Juan Manuel de. (Pp. 105, 106, 108.) Born in La Plata in 1793. He was brought up a Gaucho on the plains, and became of so much importance that in 1829 he was elected Governor of the country (Argentine Confederation). Mr. Darwin met him in 1833, on the Rio Colorado, when he was conducting in person the war against the Indians. He says:

"General Rosas intimated a wish to see me; a circumstance which I was afterward very glad of. He is a man of an extraordinary character, and has a most predominant influence in the country, which it seems probable he will use to its prosperity and advancement. ['This prophecy has turned out miserably wrong,' adds Mr. Darwin, in 1845.] He is said to be the owner of seventy-four square leagues of land, and to have about three hundred thousand head of cattle. His estates are admirably managed, and are far more productive of corn than those of others. He first gained his celebrity by his laws for his own estancias, and by disciplining several hundred men so as to resist with success the attacks of the Indians. There are many stories current about the rigid manner in which his laws were enforced. One of these was that no man, on penalty of being put into the stocks, should carry his knife on a Sunday. This being the principal day for gambling and drinking, many quarrels arose, which, from the general manner of fighting with the knife, often proved fatal. One Sunday the Governor came in great form to pay the estancia a visit, and General Rosas, in his hurry, walked out to receive him, with his knife as usual stuck in his belt. The steward touched his arm, and reminded him of the law; upon which, turning to the Governor, he said he was extremely sorry, but that he must go into the stocks, and that, till let out, he possessed no power, even in his own house. After a little time the steward was persuaded to open the stocks and to let him out; but no sooner was this done than he turned to the steward and said, 'You now have broken the laws, so you must take my place in the stocks.' Such actions as these delighted the Gauchos, who all possess high notions of their own equality and dignity.

"General Rosas is also a perfect horseman—an accomplishment of no small consequence in a country where an assembled army elected its general by the following trial: a troop of unbroken horses being driven into a corral, were let out through a gate-way above which was a crossbar; it was agreed whoever should drop from the bar on one of these wild animals, as it rushed out, and should be able, without saddle or bridle, not only to ride it, but also to bring it back to the door of the corral, should be their general. The person who succeeded was accordingly elected, and doubtless made a fit general for such an army. This extraordinary feat has also been performed by Rosas.

"By these means, and by conforming to the dress and habits of the Gauchos, he has obtained an unbounded popularity in the country, and, in consequence, a despotic power. I was assured by an English merchant that a man who had murdered another, when arrested and questioned concerning his motive, answered, 'He spoke disrespectfully of General Rosas, so I killed him.' At the end of a week the murderer was at liberty. This, doubtless, was the act of the general's party, and not of the general himself. [But subsequent events showed that it might well have been the general's act.]

"In conversation he is enthusiastic, sensible, and very grave. His gravity is carried to a high pitch. I heard one of his mad buffoons (for he keeps two, like the barons of old) relate the following anecdote: 'I wanted very much to hear a certain piece of music, so I went to the general two or three times to ask him; he said to me, "Go about your business, for I am engaged." I went a second time. He said, "If you come again I will punish you." A third time I asked, and he laughed. I rushed out of the tent, but it was too late. He ordered two soldiers to catch and stake me. I begged by all the saints in heaven he would let me off—but it would not do; when the general laughs he spares neither madman nor sound.' The poor flighty gentleman looked quite dolorous at the very recollection of the staking. This is a very severe punishment: four posts are driven into the ground, and the man is extended by his arms and legs horizontally, and then left to stretch for several hours. The idea is evidently taken from the usual method of drying hides. My interview passed away without a smile, and I obtained a passport and order for the Government post-horses, and this he gave me in the most obliging and ready manner."

In 1835 Rosas made himself dictator, and a more terrible ruler never cursed a nation. A picture of life at the capital, while this

GENERAL ROSAS.

tyrant was feared as much as he was hated and flattered, may be found in the interesting work called "Life in the Argentine Republic in the Days of the Tyrants," by D. F. Sarmiento, afterward President of the Republic, which was translated by Mrs. Horace Mann, and published in New York in 1868. This work was written some years before the downfall of the dictator, and only partly relates to him. "The Reign of Rosas; or, South American Sketches," by E. C. Fernau, was published in London in 1877. Rosas was defeated in battle by General Urquiza in 1852, and spent the remainder of his days in exile, dying in England in March, 1877.

Sturt, CHARLES. (Page 72.) An English officer, captain of the 39th Regiment; born 1795; died June 16th, 1869, at Cheltenham, England. In 1828–31 he explored the great basin of the Murray River in South-eastern Australia, of which the Murrumbidgee is a tributary. In 1844–46 he penetrated nearly to the centre of the continent. Of these journeys he gave an account in "Two Expeditions into the Interior of Southern Australia" (London, 1833), and "Narrative of an Exploration into Central Australia" (London, 1849).

Symonds, WILLIAM. (Page 76.) An English rear-admiral and naval architect; born 1782; died 1856.

GENERAL INDEX.

*** The pronunciation of the more difficult FOREIGN NAMES is indicated in parentheses (ā as in *fate*; ē as in *equal*; ī as in *like*; ō as in *tone*; *oo* as in *food*). When not indicated, the chief thing to remember is, that *a* generally sounds as in *father*, *e* like *a* in *fate*, *i* like *e* in *equal*, *u* like *oo* in *food*.

Span. = Spanish; Port. = Portuguese; Fr. = French; Ger. = German; Dan. = Danish; Eng. = English.

A.

B.

D.

E.

I.

J.

K.

L.

P.

Q.

R.

Y.

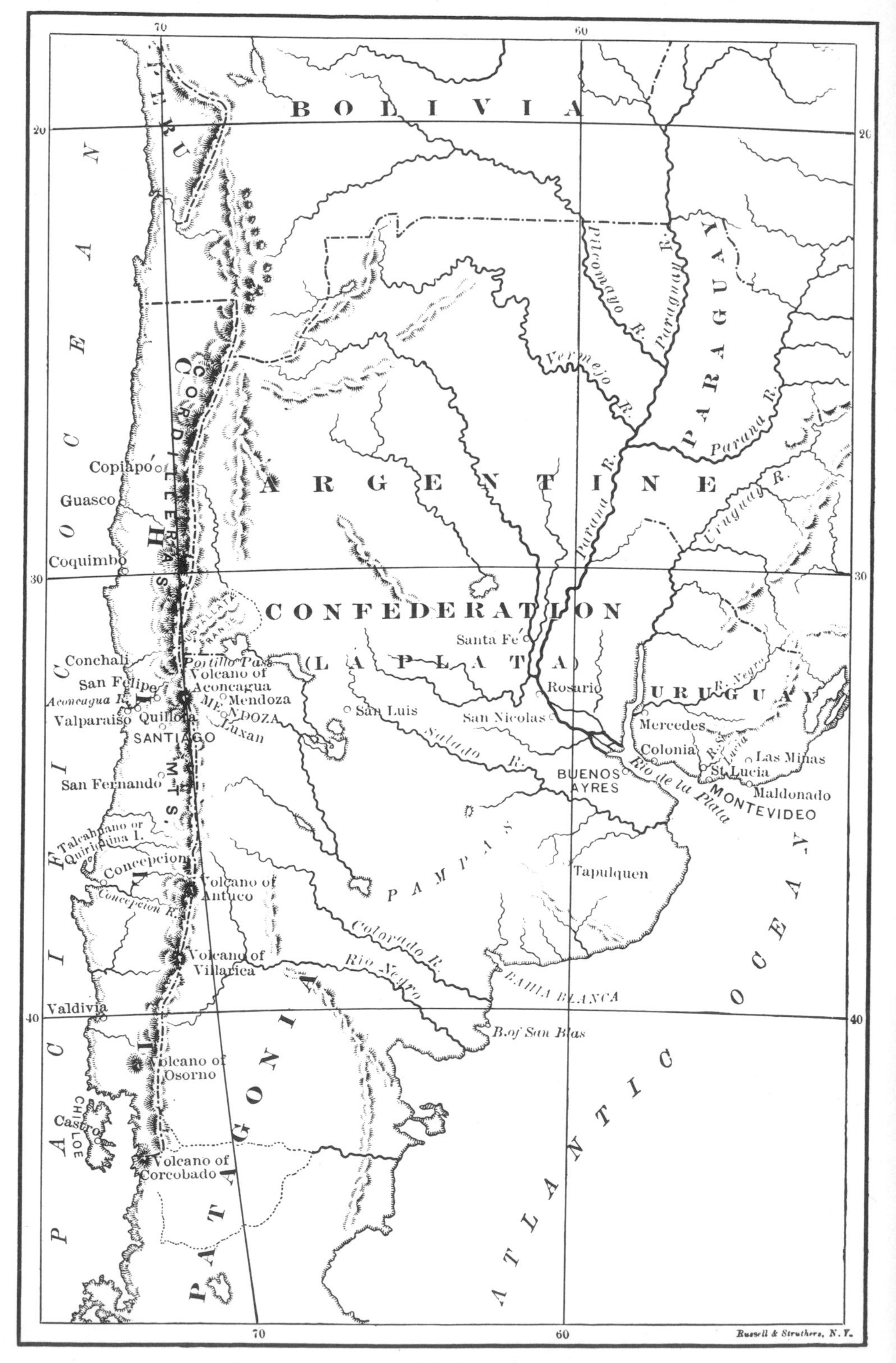

CHILE, ARGENTINE CONFEDERATION, URUGUAY.